The Adventures of Pinocchio

by Carlo Collodi

Level 2
(1300-word)

Retold by Marie Hunter

IBC パブリッシング

はじめに

　ラダーシリーズは、「はしご（ladder）」を使って一歩一歩上を目指すように、学習者の実力に合わせ、無理なくステップアップできるよう開発された英文リーダーのシリーズです。

　リーディング力をつけるためには、繰り返したくさん読むこと、いわゆる「多読」がもっとも効果的な学習法であると言われています。多読では、「1. 速く 2. 訳さず英語のまま 3. なるべく辞書を使わず」に読むことが大切です。スピードを計るなど、速く読むよう心がけましょう（たとえば TOEIC® テストの音声スピードはおよそ 1 分間に 150語です）。そして 1 語ずつ訳すのではなく、英語を英語のまま理解するくせをつけるようにします。こうして読み続けるうちに語感がついてきて、だんだんと英語が理解できるようになるのです。まずは、ラダーシリーズの中からあなたのレベルに合った本を選び、少しずつ英文に慣れ親しんでください。たくさんの本を手にとるうちに、英文書がすらすら読めるようになってくるはずです。

《本シリーズの特徴》

- 中学校レベルから中級者レベルまで5段階に分かれています。自分に合ったレベルからスタートしてください。
- クラシックから現代文学、ノンフィクション、ビジネスと幅広いジャンルを扱っています。あなたの興味に合わせてタイトルを選べます。
- 巻末のワードリストで、いつでもどこでも単語の意味を確認できます。レベル1、2では、文中の全ての単語が、レベル3以上は中学校レベル外の単語が掲載されています。
- カバーにヘッドホーンマークのついているタイトルは、オーディオ・サポートがあります。ウェブから購入／ダウンロードし、リスニング教材としても併用できます。

《使用語彙について》

レベル1：中学校で学習する単語約1000語

レベル2：レベル1の単語＋使用頻度の高い単語約300語

レベル3：レベル1の単語＋使用頻度の高い単語約600語

レベル4：レベル1の単語＋使用頻度の高い単語約1000語

レベル5：語彙制限なし

The Adventures of
Pinocchio

登場人物紹介

Pinocchio ピノキオ

ゼペットに作られた操り人形。心を持ち、ものを感じ、自分で動くことができる。やさしい心を持っているが、怠け癖があって誘惑に弱い。

Geppetto ゼペット

貧しい木工彫刻家。ピノキオの生みの親。言うことを聞かない不孝者のピノキオをわが子のように愛している。

Contents

Chapter 1 .... *1*

Chapter 2 .... *4*

Chapter 3 .... *7*

Chapter 4 .... *10*

Chapter 5 .... *13*

Chapter 6 .... *16*

Chapter 7 .... *20*

Chapter 8 .... *25*

Chapter 9 .... *31*

Chapter 10 .... *37*

Chapter 11 .... *41*

Chapter 12 .... *47*

Fairy フェアリー

青い髪の美しい乙女の姿をした妖精。
ピノキオの母親的存在となる。

Chapter 13 53	本書で使われている用語です。わからない語は巻末のワードリストで確認しましょう。
Chapter 14 60	
Chapter 15 66	
Chapter 16 71	☐ aid
Chapter 17 77	☐ carve
Chapter 18 81	☐ deserve
Chapter 19 85	☐ disobedient
Chapter 20 90	☐ donkey
Chapter 21 95	☐ jail
Chapter 22 105	☐ lame
	☐ lazy
Word List 110	☐ marionette
	☐ mischief
	☐ piece
	☐ shiver
	☐ shore
	☐ straw
	☐ strength
	☐ swallow

Cricket クリケット

ゼペットの家に100年以上も暮らしている、人語を解する賢いコオロギ。

Lamp-Wick ランプウィック

ピノキオのお気に入りの友人。怠け者の悪童。

Chapter 1

Once upon a time there was a block of wood. This block of wood was not just any block of wood—it was a block of wood that thought and felt things, much like a real human could. But how can this be, you ask? Let me tell you the story of Pinocchio.

One day, a wood carver named Geppetto decided to make himself a Marionette. He would call him Pinocchio. Geppetto imagined traveling the world with this puppet—making it dance, sing, and perform in theaters everywhere. He would earn his living from Pinocchio's performances, making enough money for food and shelter as he traveled.

As Geppetto began to carve this block of wood, creating eyes, a nose, and a mouth, the wood began to laugh and tease Geppetto. Geppetto could not believe his eyes! He was sure he was imagining it, so he continued carving. But as soon as he had carved two legs for the Marionette, the Marionette jumped up, and ran away!

CHAPTER 1

Out the door Pinocchio ran on his new wooden legs. "Catch him, catch him!" Geppetto shouted as he chased Pinocchio through the small village streets. Now, Geppetto was known all over his village for his terrible temper, so naturally everyone who saw the chase was sure that Pinocchio was running to escape Geppetto's anger. "Catch him! Catch him!" Geppetto continued to cry, as Pinocchio ran farther and faster. A policeman began to run after Geppetto. He, too, was sure that Pinocchio should be free, and that it was Geppetto who deserved to go to jail.

Chapter 2

The policeman caught Geppetto. "I am bringing you straight to jail!" he said. Pinocchio could not believe his luck—he was free! He ran back to Geppetto's home, and once inside, he heard a noise.

"What is that? Who is there?" asked Pinocchio, scared.

He looked around and saw it was a tiny talking cricket. "I must tell you a great truth," said the wise old cricket, who said he had been living in Geppetto's house for 100 years. "Boys who refuse to obey their parents will never be happy in this world. When they are older, they will be very sorry for it."

"I am not like regular boys and girls who

CHAPTER 2

go to school and must study," Pinocchio told the cricket. "I am meant to run around and play and climb trees. I am meant to be free!" Pinocchio said cheerfully.

But the cricket would not listen. "If you do not like school, why don't you at least learn a trade, so that you can earn money?"

"There is only one job I could have," said Pinocchio.

"What is that?"

"Eating, drinking, sleeping, and playing all day, from morning to night."

"Silly boy!" said the cricket. "Those who do that only wind up in the hospital or in jail."

"Don't make me angry!" cried Pinocchio. "If you make me angry, you'll be sorry."

"Oh Pinocchio," said the cricket. "I am sorry for you, for you are only a marionette, and you have a wooden head."

Pinocchio grew so angry upon hearing this that he took a hammer, and threw it with all his strength. He smashed the poor cricket to death.

Chapter 3

Alone once again in the quiet of the house, Pinocchio realized he was very hungry. He set off in search of food, but after several hours returned home with his stomach still empty. He was tired and freezing cold. As he tried to warm his feet on a stove, he fell asleep. He was so tired, he did not feel his feet burn off.

Suddenly he heard knocking at the door. "Who is it?" he called.

"It is I," answered the voice. It was the voice of Geppetto! "Open the door!"

"Dear Father, dear Father, I can't," answered Pinocchio. "I have no feet!"

Geppetto thought this was another one of

his puppet's tricks, so he climbed in through the window. When he saw that Pinocchio really had no feet, he felt very sad. Picking him up from the floor, he hugged him and said, "My little Pinocchio, how did you burn your feet?"

"I don't know, Father, but believe me, this night has been terrible, and I shall remember it forever." Pinocchio began to cry. Geppetto, feeling sorry for him, pulled fruit out of his pocket.

"This fruit was my breakfast, but I give it to you," he said gently to his boy. Pinocchio ate it up.

Once he was no longer hungry, Pinocchio asked Geppetto for new feet.

"Why should I make your feet over again? To see you run away from home once more?" asked Geppetto.

"I promise you that from now on I will be

Chapter 3

good..." Pinocchio said.

"Boys always promise that when they want something," said Geppetto.

"I'm telling the truth," Pinocchio insisted. "I will go to school, study, and find a job! I will take care of you in your old age."

Geppetto felt bad for Pinocchio, for he was so unhappy, so he set to work to make his boy a new pair of legs.

With his new legs, Pinocchio was ready to start school.

Chapter 4

Geppetto was very poor. He had no money to buy his son school books, but he wanted very much for Pinocchio to go to school so that he could learn and then go to work. He decided to sell his own winter coat, so that he could give Pinocchio the money to buy his books. Pinocchio was very thankful for the old man's good heart. He set off to buy his books, and promised to go right to school as soon as he had bought them. Along the way, he heard the sounds of music and a drum. "Dum! Dum! Dum!" went the drums.

Pinocchio walked toward the sound, eager to find out where it was coming from. As he walked, it grew louder and louder. Finally, he

CHAPTER 4

found where it was coming from: a building that said "Great Marionette Theater."

"When did the show start?" Pinocchio asked a boy outside.

"It is starting now. It costs four pennies to get in."

Pinocchio had exactly four pennies in his pocket—the pennies he was supposed to be using for his school books. Without giving it any thought, he gave the boy his four pennies and went inside.

The performance began, and suddenly a Marionette in the play stopped talking and shouted, "Look! It's Pinocchio! Pinocchio, come here! You are my brother!"

Upon hearing such loving words, Pinocchio jumped onto the stage. How this made the play's director angry! How could Pinocchio interrupt their play? With great skill, Pinocchio was able to calm down the director.

He told the director the sad story of how Geppetto had sold his own coat for Pinocchio to buy books, and how as he walked to buy his books, he could not help but follow the sound of the beautiful drums and music. The director, touched by Pinocchio's story, gave Pinocchio five gold coins to return home and give back to his Father.

Chapter 5

Pinocchio set out to return home. Along the way, he came upon a lame fox and a blind cat. "Do you want to double your gold pieces?" the fox asked.

"What do you mean?"

"Come with us, and we'll show you," said the fox.

"No, I don't want to go. Home is near, and I'm going where Father is waiting for me. How unhappy he must be that I have not yet returned! I have been a bad son, and that cricket was right to tell me that a boy who makes mischief cannot be happy in this world."

"You'll be sorry," said the cat. "If you come with us, you can turn your five gold pieces into two thousand. Just outside the city, there is a field called the Field of Wonders. Here, if you bury your gold, it will turn into thousands of pieces."

Pinocchio thought long and hard. He thought about how, if he had two thousand gold pieces, there would be money for winter coats, and school books, and so much else. "Let us go!" Pinocchio agreed.

As they walked, night fell. Suddenly, Pinocchio saw a light. "I am the ghost of the

CHAPTER 5

talking cricket," said the light. "Follow my advice. Return home and give the gold to your Father who is crying, for he has not seen you for many days. These animals are liars. Listen to me and go home! This road is dangerous. Remember that boys who insist on having their own way, sooner or later pay the price."

"That is nonsense," Pinocchio insisted. Then there was nothing but silence, and it was dark all around him.

Chapter 6

As Pinocchio continued, he heard a noise of leaves behind him. He turned to look, and there behind him were two huge shadows, dressed head to foot in black. "Your money or your life!" the voices shouted.

Pinocchio ran for his life, through a forest full of trees and brush. In the distance, he saw a tiny house. He ran faster than he ever thought possible, and as soon as he came to the house's front door, he knocked loudly.

A window opened, and a lovely maiden with deep blue hair and a white face looked out. "No one lives here," she spoke. "Everyone is dead."

"Won't you open the door for me?"

Pinocchio said quickly. Suddenly the men in shadows, who clearly wanted to kill Pinocchio, had come upon him. They tied him up with a rope around his neck, and as he hung, he was sure he would die.

The lovely blue maiden, however, saw the whole thing. She ordered others in the forest to help Pinocchio, and they brought him to her. He was nearly dead, but the maiden called upon those who were helping her to ask whether he deserved to live or die.

"Do you hold any opinion about whether this boy should live or die?" she asked the talking cricket, who had appeared at the house.

"That Marionette," said the cricket. "is the worst kind of boy. He has no manners and is lazy. He is a disobedient son who is breaking his Father's heart!"

Pinocchio, though barely able to move, felt

his face burn in shame. The Fairy felt bad for Pinocchio, however, and she decided to give him medicine to save his life.

As he got his strength back, she asked him how he came to find himself in such trouble. He told her everything—how he had lost his Father's money, how he had disobeyed and followed the cat and fox, although he knew he shouldn't.

"Where are the gold pieces now?" the Fairy asked him.

"I lost them," answered Pinocchio. But he had told a lie, for he had the gold coins in his pocket. As he spoke, his nose grew at least two inches longer.

"Where did you lose them?" she asked.

"In the wood nearby." With this second lie, his nose grew longer still.

"If you lost them in the nearby wood, we will look for them and find them. We always

CHAPTER 6

find everything we lose there," she said.

"Now I remember," Pinocchio replied. "I did not lose the pieces. I swallowed them when I drank the medicine."

At this third lie, Pinocchio's nose became so long that he could not turn around without knocking it into something.

The Fairy began to laugh. "Why do you laugh?" asked Pinocchio.

"I am laughing at your lies, dear boy," said the Fairy. "Lies are known in a moment. There are two kinds of lies—lies with short legs and lies with long noses. Yours, just now, happen to have long noses."

Pinocchio hung his head in shame, but as he did so, his nose, which had become so long, hit the floor, and he could not escape her.

Chapter 7

The Fairy felt Pinocchio had learned his lesson. She called in woodpeckers to peck his nose down to its regular size.

"You are so good to me, dear Fairy," said Pinocchio, who could once more move his head without fear of hitting his nose.

Chapter 7

"I love you, too," answered the Fairy. "Now go to your Father, and don't lose your way."

Not long after Pinocchio had set out, he came upon the fox and cat once again. They asked him yet again to follow them to the Field of Wonders.

Pinocchio thought for a moment, as he not only remembered the promise he'd made to Geppetto, but also the advice of the cricket and the good Fairy. Still, he could not resist. "Let us go! I am with you!" And off they went.

They walked and walked, until they could walk no further. Finally, they came upon the Field of Wonders.

"Here we are," said the fox to Pinocchio. "Dig a hole here and put in your gold pieces. Cover it up, and then go to the nearby river. There, fill a bucket with water, return here, and put some water over this spot. As soon as the ground has been watered, walk away. Return in 20 minutes, and upon your return, you will find a small tree, and branches filled with gold pieces!"

Pinocchio, beside himself with joy, thanked the fox and followed his instructions. Twenty minutes could not pass quickly enough. Finally, he returned to the field, hoping to see a tree of gold in the distance. As he got closer, he saw no tree. He looked all around the field—no tree!

He heard laughter above his head. There, just above him on the branch of a regular tree, sat a large parrot. "Why are you laughing?" asked Pinocchio.

"I am laughing at simple boys like you who believe everything you hear!" the parrot laughed. "You are so easily caught in the traps others set up for you!" the parrot continued. "You are so silly to think that gold

CHAPTER 7

can be grown in a field like this. Don't you know? In order to come by money, you must work and know how to earn it with hand or brain! Money doesn't grow on trees!"

"I don't know what you're talking about," Pinocchio said, knowing deep down exactly what the parrot was talking about.

"While you were away, waiting for this tree to grow, a fox and cat returned to this very spot, dug in the ground, picked up your gold pieces, and ran away!" The parrot continued to laugh. "I am laughing so hard because I, too, once believed what you believed—that you could make money with no work. I now know that one must earn money only through hard work and with thought."

Pinocchio was so upset he ran away to the courthouse to report the robbery. Pinocchio stood before the judge and told him what happened. The judge listened carefully, but much to Pinocchio's surprise, when Pinocchio finished talking, the judge said, "This poor boy has been robbed of four gold pieces. Take him and throw him into jail." Pinocchio could not believe his ears.

Chapter 8

Poor Pinocchio stayed in jail for four long months. When he was finally free, he left the city to set out to find the Fairy. As he walked, he thought, "How unhappy I have been. And yet I deserve everything! For I certainly have not used my head! I always have my own way. I don't listen to those who love me and who have more brains than I. From now on, I will be different, and I will try to become an obedient boy. I find that disobedient boys are certainly far from happy, and in the long run, they always lose out."

He finally came upon the spot where the Fairy's house had once stood. Much to his

THE ADVENTURES OF PINOCCHIO

sadness, the house was gone, and only a sign was left that said:

Here Lies
The Lovely Fairy
Who Died of Sadness
When Left By
Her Little Brother Pinocchio

These words broke Pinocchio's heart. He cried loudly, "Oh my Fairy! Why did you die? Why did I not die, who am so bad, instead of you, who are so good? And my Father—where can he be? You are not really dead, are you?"

Suddenly, a large pigeon flew down and asked him, "Do you know a Marionette named Pinocchio?"

"Pinocchio! Did you say Pinocchio? Why I am Pinocchio!" Pinocchio exclaimed.

Chapter 8

"Then you must know Geppetto?" asked the pigeon.

"Of course I know him—he is my Father! Do you know where he is?" Pinocchio asked, feeling very excited.

"I left him three days ago on the shore of a large sea. He was building a little boat with which to cross the ocean. I can take you to him."

Pinocchio got on board the pigeon's strong back, and away they flew. Suddenly they spotted Geppetto in a little boat, being thrown about in angry waters. When it disappeared, Pinocchio cried out, "Put me down! I will save him! I will save my Father!"

But as Pinocchio, who could float easily because he was made of wood, searched for his Father, night fell. He swam all night long, but still saw no sign of him. When he reached land, he realized he was starving, for it had been a very long time since he ate. He came upon an old woman who gave him some work in exchange for food.

Having completed his work, Pinocchio sat down for his food. As he ate, he looked up at the kind woman, and noticed she looked like someone else he knew. "You, you, you…" Pinocchio said. He could not get out the words.

"Why, what is it, my dear?" The kind woman asked.

"You remind me of—yes, yes, the same

CHAPTER 8

voice, the same eyes, the same hair—yes, you also have the same blue hair she had. Oh, my little Fairy! My little Fairy! Tell me that it is you! I have cried so much! I have suffered so!"

Pinocchio threw himself on the floor, took hold of her knees, and cried.

"I promise, I will be a good boy," Pinocchio cried.

"Do you promise?" she asked.

"It's not true that you're dead, is it? If only you knew how I cried!" Pinocchio said.

"I know it, and I have forgiven you. Seeing your sadness shows me you have a very kind heart, indeed. There is always hope for boys with a heart like yours. This is why I have come so far to look for you. From now, I will be your own little mother."

"Oh! How wonderful!" cried Pinocchio, jumping with joy.

29

"You must always obey me and do as I wish, though," the Fairy said. "Beginning tomorrow, you'll go to school every day. Then, you will choose a trade you like best. You must remember that, because if you do not work, 'woe betide the lazy fellow!' Laziness is a serious illness and we must cure it immediately. If not, it will kill you in the end," the Fairy said seriously.

"I promise," said Pinocchio. "I will study. I will work. I will do all that you ask. I promise."

Chapter 9

Pinocchio kept his promise and went to school the very next day. While he was teased by his classmates because he was just a Marionette, Pinocchio kept his head down and continued with his studies. Even his teacher told him how well he was doing, for he saw Pinocchio as wanting to learn and always working hard—he was always the first to get to school, and the last to leave.

As school continued, Pinocchio proved himself to his classmates, and they slowly became his friends. His friends, however, were bad boys who did not care for school. He tried to keep his head down, and his mind on school, but his friends continued to

try to get him to leave school.

One day they told him a shark as big as a mountain was discovered near the shore, and they tried to get Pinocchio to come see it. Pinocchio never could find Geppetto, and he had heard about this shark near the spot he'd last seen his Father. He decided to follow them, only to find they had been lying—there was no shark near the shore.

A terrible fight broke out between

CHAPTER 9

Pinocchio and his friends. They began throwing heavy school books, and one of his friends threw one of Pinocchio's books very hard. It hit one of Pinocchio's friends, Eugene, on the head. Poor Eugene fell on the ground, crying out, "Help! I'm dying!" The boys all ran away, leaving only Pinocchio to tend to Eugene.

When two policemen came to their aid, Pinocchio knew how all of this looked. A boy lay dying, struck by a book. Pinocchio was the only person around, and it was clear it was Pinocchio's book that struck Eugene. Although Pinocchio cried, "It was not me! I did not do it!", the policemen did not believe him. "Come with us!" the policemen said.

Before starting out, the officers called out to several fishermen passing by in a boat and said to them:

"Take care of this boy who has been hurt.

Take him home and tend to his wounds. Tomorrow we will come for him."

The policemen then took hold of Pinocchio, and said to him, "March! And go quickly, or it will be worse for you!"

Pinocchio did not need to be told twice. He walked quickly along the road, but inside he felt sick. He was seeing double, his legs shook, his tongue was dry. He could not speak. Yet, despite all of this, he thought of

CHAPTER 9

his Fairy: What would she think?

A sudden wind blew Pinocchio's hat off of his head. "Would you allow me," Pinocchio asked the policemen, "to run after my hat?"

"Very well," they replied. "But hurry!"

Pinocchio ran after his hat, picked it up, and instead of putting it on his head, put it between his teeth and ran to the sea.

The police, judging that it would be very hard to catch him, sent a large dog after him. Pinocchio ran as if his life depended on it, as fast as his wooden legs could carry him. The dog was just a few steps away from him, but luckily he had come upon the beach. The sea was just a few short steps away, and once he was upon it, Pinocchio dove into the sea.

The dog followed him. As strange as it may seem, the dog could not swim. While Pinocchio was greatly relieved the dog could no longer get him—Pinocchio was a wonderful swimmer, after all—he saw the panic on the dog's face. The dog barked, as he said, "Help me! Help!"

"No!" answered Pinocchio, so happy he had gotten away.

"Help, Pinocchio! Dear Pinocchio! Save me!"

Upon hearing these cries, Pinocchio, who had a very kind heart, could not let the dog drown. He turned toward the poor animal and said to him, "If I help you, will you promise not to chase me again?"

"I promise! I promise! Hurry! If you wait another second, I will die!"

Pinocchio waited a second more. Then, remembering how Geppetto told him a kind deed is never lost, he swam to the dog, caught him by the tail, and brought him to the shore.

Chapter 10

Pinocchio swam back out to sea. Suddenly he was being pulled up out of the water in a huge net. To his surprise, he was squeezed in with all kinds of fish, who were fighting to free themselves.

A Fisherman took the net, and said "Hurray! I shall have a fine meal of fish!"

"Thank God I am not a fish!" said Pinocchio to himself.

The Fisherman took the net and the fish to a little spot where he had a fire going and a pan on which to cook the fish. "Let's see what kinds of fish I have caught today," said the Fisherman. He put his hand in the net and pulled out some mullets.

"What fine mullets!" he said, looking at them and smelling them with pleasure. After that, he threw them into a large, empty tub.

He repeated this over and over. "Fine fish, these bass!"

"Very good, these whitefish!"

"What wonderful crabs!"

The last to come out of the net was Pinocchio. As soon as the Fisherman pulled him out, his green eyes opened wide with surprise, and he cried out in fear:

"What kind of fish is this? I don't remember ever eating anything like it."

He looked at him carefully, and after turning him over and over, he said at last:

"I understand. He must be a crab!"

Pinocchio could not believe the Fisherman thought he was a crab, and said:

"What nonsense! I am not a crab! I am a Marionette!"

CHAPTER 10

"A Marionette?" asked the Fisherman. "A Marionette seems like a fish to me. I shall eat you! You look delicious."

"Eat me? But can't you understand that I'm not a fish? Can't you hear that I speak and think as you do?"

"It's true," answered the Fisherman; "but since I see that you are a fish, well able to talk and think as I do, I will treat you with respect. You may choose how I cook you. Do you wish to be cooked plain in a pan, or do you prefer to be cooked with tomato sauce?"

"To tell you the truth," answered Pinocchio, "I much prefer to go free so I may return home!"

"Are you joking? I will not. I shall cook you in the pan with the others."

The unlucky Marionette, hearing this, began to cry. With tears running down his cheeks, he said:

"How much better it would have been for me to go to school! I did listen to my friends and now I am paying for it! Oh! Oh! Oh!"

As he struggled to escape, the Fisherman took some rope, tied his hands and feet together, and threw him in the tub with the other fish.

He pulled down a wooden bowl filled with flour, and he began to cover the fish in it, one by one. When they were white with flour, he threw them into the pan. The first to dance in the hot oil were the mullets, the bass followed, then the crabs. Pinocchio's turn came last. Seeing himself so near to death (and such a terrible death!) he began to shake so hard with fear that he had no voice left.

The Fisherman picked up Pinocchio next, and turned him over and over in the flour, until you could hardly see his face. Then he took him by the head and...

Chapter 11

Pinocchio knew all hope was gone. He closed his eyes and waited for the final moment.

Suddenly, a large Dog smelled the Fisherman's cooking and came running over.

"Get out!" cried the Fisherman, still holding onto the Marionette, who was all covered with flour.

But the poor Dog was very hungry. He said:

"Give me a bite of the fish and I will go in peace."

"Get out, I say!" repeated the Fisherman.

Then the Dog, who, being really hungry,

would not accept this answer, turned in anger toward the Fisherman and showed his scary teeth. At that moment, Pinocchio realized this was the same dog whose life he had just saved. "Save me, friend! If you don't, I die!"

CHAPTER 11

The Dog immediately recognized Pinocchio's voice. He could not believe the voice came from the little flour-covered figure that the Fisherman held in his hand.

So what did the dog do? With one great jump forward, he took the figure out of the Fisherman's hand, held it between his teeth, and ran like the wind!

As soon as the dog came upon the road that led to the village, he stopped and dropped Pinocchio softly to the ground.

"Thank you! Oh, thank you!" said the Marionette.

"It is not necessary," answered the Dog. "You saved me once, and what is given is always returned. We are in this world to help one another."

"But how did you get in there?"

"I was lying here on the beach more dead than alive, when a lovely smell of fish came to me. I followed it. Oh, if I had come a moment later!"

"Don't speak about it," cried Pinocchio, still shaking with fear. "Don't say a word. If you had come a moment later, I would be dead. I shiver at the thought of it!"

The dog laughed and held out his paw to Pinocchio to shake it. They said good-bye to one another, knowing that now they were good friends.

Pinocchio, left alone, walked toward a little house nearby, where an old man sat at the door, and asked:

"Tell me, good man, have you heard anything of a poor boy whose name was Eugene?"

"The boy was brought to this house and now—"

"Now he is dead?" Pinocchio interrupted sadly.

Chapter 11

"No, he is now alive and he has already returned home."

"Really? Really?" cried the Marionette, jumping around with joy. "Then the wound was not serious?"

"It could have been," answered the old man, "for a heavy book was thrown at his head."

"And who threw it?"

"A friend of his, a certain Pinocchio."

"And who is this Pinocchio?" asked the Marionette, pretending he knew nothing of this event.

"They say he is a mischief-maker. Do you know him?"

"Only by sight," answered the Marionette.

"And what do you think of him?" asked the old man.

"I think he's a very good boy, he likes school, he's very obedient, and very kind to his Father and family," Pinocchio said.

As he was telling all these very big lies about himself, Pinocchio touched his nose and it was twice as long as it should be. Scared, he cried out:

"Actually, don't listen to me, good man! All the wonderful things I have said are not true at all. I know Pinocchio well and he is indeed a bad boy, lazy and disobedient, who instead of going to school, runs away to have a good time."

Suddenly, his nose returned to its regular size.

Pinocchio decided to start out for the village. As he walked he said to himself:

"How shall I ever face my good little Fairy? What will she say when she sees me?"

Chapter 12

He came to the village late at night. It was so dark he could see nothing, and it was pouring rain.

Pinocchio went straight to the Fairy's house, and stood at the door. But he could not find the courage to knock. He ran back a few steps. He went back to the door, then ran back again. A third time he did this. The fourth time, before he had time to lose his courage, he knocked on the door.

He waited and waited and waited. Finally, after a full half hour, a window opened and Pinocchio saw a large Snail look out. "Who knocks at this late hour?" she called.

"Is the Fairy home?" asked the Marionette.

"The Fairy is asleep and does not wish for anyone to bother her. Who are you?"

"It is I."

"Who's I?"

"Pinocchio."

"Who is Pinocchio?"

"The Marionette; the one who lives in the Fairy's house."

"Oh, I understand," said the Snail. "Wait for me there. I will come down to open the door for you."

"Hurry, I am freezing cold."

"My boy, I am a snail and snails are never in a hurry."

An hour passed, two hours; and the door was still closed. Pinocchio, who was shaking with fear and shivering from the cold rain, knocked a second time, this time louder than before.

At that second knock, a window on the

CHAPTER 12

third floor opened and the same Snail looked out.

"Dear little Snail," cried Pinocchio. "I have been waiting two hours for you! Hurry, please!"

"My boy," answered the Snail in a calm, peaceful voice, "my dear boy, I am a snail and snails are never in a hurry." And the window closed.

Two more hours passed, and still, the door stayed closed!

Then Pinocchio, who could wait no longer, kicked in the door. His foot went through, but still, it would not open. There he waited for hours, with one foot inside the house, and one foot out. He was trapped. As morning came, the door finally opened. That brave little animal, the Snail, had taken exactly nine hours to come to the door.

"What are you doing with your foot

through the door?" she asked the Marionette, laughing.

"It was an accident. Please ask the Fairy to help me!" Pinocchio said.

"The Fairy is asleep and does not want to be woken up."

"But what do you want me to do, stuck in the door like this?"

"Look at bugs on the ground."

"Please bring me something to eat, at least, for I am starving," Pinocchio said.

"Immediately!"

Of course, for the snail, immediately took three and a half hours. Pinocchio finally saw her return with a silver plate on her head. On the plate was bread, chicken, and fruit.

"Here is the breakfast the Fairy sends to you," said the Snail.

At the sight of all these good things, the Marionette felt much better.

CHAPTER 12

But upon tasting the food, he discovered the bread was made of paper, the chicken of wood, and the fruit was plastic!

He wanted to cry, but whether it was from pain or weakness, he fell to the floor and fainted.

When he woke up, he was stretched out on a bed. The Fairy was next to him.

"I forgive you this last time," the Fairy said to him. "But you must promise not to make trouble again."

Pinocchio promised to study and to do everything that was asked of him. And he kept his word for the rest of the year. He passed first in all his tests, and his report was so good that the Fairy said to him, smiling:

"Tomorrow your wish will come true."

"And what is it?"

"Tomorrow you will no longer be a Marionette. You will become a real boy."

Pinocchio could not contain his joy. He must invite all his friends to celebrate the great event! The Fairy promised to prepare two hundred cups of coffee and four hundred pieces of toast with butter on them.

The day promised to be very happy, but—

Unluckily, in Pinocchio's life there is always a "but" which spoils everything.

Chapter 13

"Can I invite my friends to celebrate?" Pinocchio asked.

"Yes, you may invite your friends to tomorrow's party. Only remember to return home before dark. Do you understand?"

"I will be back in one hour, I promise," answered the Marionette.

"Take care, Pinocchio! Boys give promises very easily, but they as easily forget them."

"But I am not like those others. When I give my word I keep it."

"We shall see. Just remember, that if you do disobey, it is only you who will pay the price."

"Why?"

"Because boys who do not listen to their elders always pay the price."

"I certainly have," said Pinocchio, "but from now on, I obey."

"We will see if you are telling the truth."

Without adding another word, the Marionette said good-bye to the Fairy, and he left the house singing and dancing.

In a little more than an hour, all his friends, except one, were invited. He had saved his favorite friend for last. The boy's name was Lamp-Wick.

Lamp-Wick was the laziest boy in the school and the biggest mischief-maker, but Pinocchio loved him like a brother.

That day, he went straight to his friend's house to invite him to the party, but Lamp-Wick was not at home. He went a second time, and again a third, but still without success.

CHAPTER 13

Where could he be? Pinocchio searched everywhere and finally discovered him hiding near a farmer's wagon.

"What are you doing there?" asked Pinocchio, running up to him.

"I am waiting for midnight to go—"

"Where?"

"Far, far away!"

"I have gone to your house three times to look for you!"

"What do you want from me?"

"Haven't you heard the news?"

"What?"

"Tomorrow I end my days as a Marionette and become a boy, like you and all my other friends. Can you come to my party tomorrow?"

"But I am leaving tonight."

"At what time?"

"At midnight."

THE ADVENTURES OF PINOCCHIO

"And where are you going?"

"To a real country—the best in the world—a wonderful place!"

"What is it called?"

"It is called the Land of Toys. Why don't you come, too?"

"I? Oh, no!"

"You are making a big mistake, Pinocchio. Believe me, if you don't come, you'll be sorry. In this wonderful place there are no schools, no teachers, no books! Every day, except Sunday, is like a Saturday! Vacation begins on the first of January and ends on the last day of December. We would be so happy!"

"But how does one spend the day in the Land of Toys?"

"Days are spent playing and laughing from morning to night. When you go to bed and wake up in the morning, the good times begin all over again. What do you say?"

CHAPTER 13

"Hmm," said Pinocchio, thinking. "It certainly sounds like a wonderful life."

"Do you want to go with me, then? Yes or no? You must make up your mind."

"No, no, and again no! I have promised my kind Fairy to become a good boy, and I want to keep my word. The sun is setting, and I must leave you and run. Good-bye and good luck to you!"

"Where are you going in such a hurry?"

"Home. My good Fairy wants me to return home before night."

"Wait two minutes more."

"It's too late!"

"Only two minutes."

"And if the Fairy is angry?"

"Let her get angry. After she gets tired, she will stop," said Lamp-Wick.

"Are you going alone or with others?"

"Alone? There will be more than a hundred

The Adventures of Pinocchio

of us!"

"No, no. I want to return home. I have waited too long as it is. The Fairy will be worried."

"Poor Fairy! What is she afraid of if you are out late?"

"Listen, Lamp-Wick," said the Marionette, "are you really sure that there are no schools in the Land of Toys? Not even one teacher?"

"Not one."

"And one does not have to study?"

"Never, never, never!"

"What a great land!" said Pinocchio, feeling excited. "What a beautiful land! I have never been there, but I can well imagine it."

"Why don't you come, too?"

"I made a promise, and I am going to keep my word. Good-bye." With these words, the Marionette started on his way home. Turning once more to his friend, he asked him:

CHAPTER 13

"But are you sure that, in that country, each week has six Saturdays and one Sunday?"

"Very sure!"

"And that vacation begins on the first day of January and ends on the last day of December?"

"Very, very sure!"

"What a great country!" repeated Pinocchio. Then, he said quickly:

"Good-bye for the last time, and good luck."

"Good-bye."

In the meantime, the night became darker and darker. All at once in the distance a small light shined. A soft sound could be heard.

"There it is!" cried Lamp-Wick, jumping to his feet.

"What?" whispered Pinocchio.

"The wagon coming to get me. For the last time, are you coming or not?"

"What a wonderful, beautiful country!"

Chapter 14

The wagon arrived, with twelve pairs of donkeys pulling it. A fat, little man drove the wagon. He was round as a ball of butter.

The wagon was so packed with boys of all ages that it looked like a box of sardines. They were sitting one on top of the other, yet no one complained.

The man turned to Lamp-Wick: "Tell me, my fine boy, do you also want to come to my wonderful country?"

"Indeed I do."

"But I warn you, my little dear, there's no more room in the wagon. It is full."

"Never mind," answered Lamp-Wick. "If there's no room inside, I can sit on the top."

CHAPTER 14

"What about you, my love?" asked the Little Man, turning to Pinocchio. "What are you going to do? Will you come with us, or do you stay here?"

"I stay here," answered Pinocchio. "I want to return home, as I prefer to study and succeed in life."

"May that bring you luck!"

"Pinocchio!" Lamp-Wick called out. "Listen to me. Come with us, and we'll always be happy."

"No, no, no!"

"Come with us, and we'll always be happy," cried four other voices from the wagon.

"Come with us, and we'll always be happy," shouted the one hundred boys in the wagon, all together.

"If I go with you, what will my good Fairy say?" asked the Marionette, who was

The Adventures of Pinocchio

beginning to weaken.

"Don't worry!"

Pinocchio did not answer, but sighed once—twice—a third time. Finally, he said:

"Make room for me. I want to go, too!"

The wagon started on its way. While the donkeys galloped along the road, the Marionette heard a very quiet voice whispering to him:

"Poor silly boy! You have done as you wished. But you are going to be a sorry boy before very long."

Pinocchio, very scared, looked about him to see where the words had come from, but he saw no one.

After a mile or so, Pinocchio again heard the same voice, whispering: "Remember— Boys who stop studying and turn their backs upon books and schools and teachers in order to give all their time to nonsense and pleasure, sooner or later pay the price. Oh, how well I know this! How well I can prove it to you! A day will come when you will be sad you made this decision—but it will be too late!"

At these whispered words, the Marionette grew more and more scared. He jumped to the ground, ran up to one of the donkeys, and he saw that the donkey was crying, just like a boy!

"Hey, Mr. Driver!" cried the Marionette. "Do you know what strange thing is happening here! This donkey cries."

"Let him cry. When he gets married, he will have time to laugh."

"Have you perhaps taught him to speak?"

"No. Do not lose time over a donkey that can cry. Get up quickly and let us go. The night is cool and the road is long."

Pinocchio obeyed. The wagon started

again. Toward dawn the next morning they finally reached the Land of Toys.

This great land was completely different from any other place in the world. Everyone who lived there was a boy. The oldest was about fourteen, the youngest, eight. It was so noisy from all of the activity, you could not hear a thing. Everywhere groups of boys were gathered together. Some played games, others rode on bicycles. They jumped all over!

As soon as they had set foot in that land, Pinocchio, Lamp-Wick, and all the other boys who had traveled with them started out to explore. They walked everywhere. They became everybody's friend. Who could be happier?

With so many fun things to do, and so many parties, the hours, days, and weeks passed as quickly as can be.

"Oh, what a beautiful life this is!" said

Chapter 14

Pinocchio every time he saw Lamp-Wick.

"Was I right or wrong?" answered Lamp-Wick. "And to think you did not want to come! To think that even yesterday the idea came into your head to return home to see your Fairy and to start studying again!"

"It's true, Lamp-Wick, it's true. If today I am a really happy boy, it is all because of you."

Five months passed and the boys continued playing and enjoying themselves from morning until night, without ever seeing a book, or a desk, or a school. But, my children, there came a morning when Pinocchio woke up and there was a great surprise waiting for him, a surprise which made him feel very unhappy, as you shall see.

Chapter 15

Everyone, at one time or another, has had some surprise waiting for him. But only a few have been as surprised as Pinocchio was on one morning of his life. What was it? I will tell you, my dear little readers. When he woke up, Pinocchio put his hand up to his head and there he discovered—

Guess!

He discovered that, during the night, his ears had grown at least ten full inches!

You must know that the Marionette had very small ears, so small indeed that you could hardly see them. He went in search of

Chapter 15

a mirror, but not finding any, he just filled a bowl with water and looked at himself. There he saw what he never could have wished to see. Around his face was a pair of donkey's ears.

He began to cry, to scream, to knock his head against the wall, but the more he screamed, the longer his ears grew.

At those cries, a Dormouse came into the room. "What is the matter, dear little neighbor?"

"I am sick, my little Dormouse, very, very sick. Feel me to see if I have a fever."

"My friend," said the dormouse. "I am sorry, but you have a very bad fever."

"But what fever is it?"

"The donkey fever."

"What do you mean?" said Pinocchio.

"Within 2-3 hours, you will no longer be a Marionette, nor a boy. You shall be a real donkey, just like the ones that pull the fruit carts to market."

"What have I done? Oh, what have I done?" said Pinocchio, pulling on his new donkey ears with anger.

"What is done cannot be undone, my friend. It happens to all lazy boys who hate school and teachers and only want to play games. Sooner or later, they turn into donkeys."

Pinocchio began to cry. "Your tears are

useless, Pinocchio," said the Dormouse. "You should have thought of this before."

"This is all Lamp-Wick's fault," Pinocchio said. "I wanted to return home. I wanted to be obedient. I wanted to study and to succeed in school, but Lamp-Wick said to me, 'Why do you want to waste your time studying? Why do you want to go to school? Come with me to the Land of Toys. There we can enjoy ourselves and be happy from morning until night.'"

"And why did you follow the advice of that false friend?"

"Why? Because I am good for nothing. I should never have left that good Fairy, who loved me so well and who has been so kind to me! And by this time, I should no longer be a Marionette. I should have become a real boy, like all these friends of mine!"

Pinocchio went off angrily in search of

Lamp-Wick, and when he came upon him he could not believe his eyes. Lamp-Wick had the same two donkey ears on either side of his face! At first, they both felt sorry and ashamed. But after a time, they began to burst out laughing. As they laughed, their legs stopped working. They fell on their hands and knees and began running and jumping like donkeys around the room. Their arms turned into legs, their noses turned into donkey snouts, and their backs became covered with long gray hairs.

As they tried to cry, no human sound came out, only donkey brays.

Chapter 16

The little man who'd driven them to the Land of Toys heard their brays.

"Fine work, boys! You have brayed well, and you are ready for me to sell." He did not have to wait long for an offer. Lamp-Wick was bought by a farmer whose donkey had died the day before. Pinocchio went to the owner of a circus, who wanted to teach him to do tricks for his audiences.

Poor Pinocchio was put in a stable, his new master filling his new home with straw. Pinocchio, after tasting some, spit it out of his mouth. The manager filled it with hay instead, but Pinocchio did not like that any better.

"You don't like hay either?" the master cried angrily. "Wait, my pretty Donkey, I will teach you to like more things."

And suddenly, he took out a whip and hit the donkey hard across the legs.

Pinocchio screamed with pain and as he screamed he brayed:

"Haw! Haw! Haw! I can't eat straw!"

"Then eat the hay!" answered his master, who understood the Donkey with no trouble.

"Haw! Haw! Haw! I hate hay!"

"Do you really think that I should feed you duck or chicken?" asked the man again, even more angry.

At that second beating, Pinocchio became very quiet and said no more.

The stable door closed, and Pinocchio was left alone. He was so hungry, he decided to eat the hay. "This hay is not bad," he said to himself. "But how much happier I should be

Chapter 16

if I had studied! Just now, instead of hay, I should be eating some good bread and butter!"

Days went on, and Pinocchio tried to be patient. The master, in the meantime, taught Pinocchio the donkey how to jump, dance, and stand on his head. Pinocchio learned all of these things, but it took him three long months.

Finally, Pinocchio could do everything the master asked, and he was ready to perform. His master scheduled a show for that evening.

That night, as you can imagine, the theater was full. Everyone in the audience clapped loudly when Pinocchio entered the circus ring.

Pinocchio obeyed everything the manager asked, as the manager cracked his whip, and cried out, "Walk! Gallop! Trot!" As Pinocchio danced before the audience, he saw in front of him a beautiful woman. Around her neck she wore a necklace, with a painted picture of a Marionette on it.

"That picture is of me! That beautiful woman is my Fairy!" said Pinocchio to himself, recognizing her. He felt so happy that he tried his best to cry out:

"Oh, my Fairy! My own Fairy!"

Instead of words, he only brayed, and the audience burst out laughing. The manager whipped Pinocchio again, and Pinocchio sadly closed his eyes. When he looked up

CHAPTER 16

again, he saw that the Fairy had disappeared! He was so sad that he could not jump through the manager's rings. In fact, as he jumped, his back legs got caught, and he fell, injured, to the ground. His legs would not work, and he could barely get off the stage.

"Pinocchio! We want Pinocchio! We want the little Donkey!" cried the audience.

No one saw Pinocchio again that evening.

The next morning the veterinary—that is, the animal doctor—told Pinocchio that he would be lame for the rest of his life.

"What do I want with a lame donkey?" said the Manager. "I shall sell him."

The manager took Pinocchio to the market, and a man asked, "How much do you ask for that little lame Donkey?"

"Four dollars."

"I will give you four cents. I want only his

skin. I can use it to make a drumhead. I need a drum."

You can imagine how upset this made Pinocchio. Right away, the man took Pinocchio to a high cliff, and pushed him off the edge into the sea below. He planned to wait for Pinocchio to drown so that he could then skin Pinocchio, and turn his skin into a drumhead.

Chapter 17

Poor Pinocchio sank deeper and deeper into the sea. The man waited a little, and then pulled the rope he had tied to Pinocchio's leg. At last Pinocchio came up to the top of the water. Do you know what the man discovered? Instead of a dead donkey, he saw a Marionette, which was very much alive!

"But I threw a donkey into the sea!" the man exclaimed.

"I am that Donkey," answered the Marionette laughing.

"You?"

"Yes, dear master."

"But how is that possible?"

"Get this rope off of my leg so I can tell

you my story."

The old man was interested to hear more. So he took off the rope, and Pinocchio began to tell his story:

"Once upon a time, I was a wooden Marionette, just as I am today. I was going to become a real boy, but because I am lazy, and I hate books, I followed the bad advice from one of my mischievous friends, and I ran away from home. I woke up one day to find I had changed into a donkey. It was a terrible day! I was taken to a fair and sold to a circus owner who whipped me and made me dance. I fell and became lame. Since I was lame, the circus owner sold me to you, and here I am."

"I sure did buy you. And I bought you for four cents. Now who will return my money to me? Where shall I find another skin to make my drumhead?"

CHAPTER 17

"Oh, dear master. There are so many donkeys in this world."

"Tell me, boy, does your story end here?"

"Well, after buying me, you brought me here to kill me. I am so happy you sent me to the bottom of the sea—I can tell you did not want me to suffer. That was very kind of you. I have a Fairy who watches over me, and..."

"Your Fairy? Who is she?"

"She is my mother, and she saved me, even though I did not deserve it. She watches over me, and she sent a thousand fishes to me deep in the sea. They began to eat me, until they got to what they thought were my bones. My bones, however, were actually my wood! Under my donkey skin, I was still a Marionette inside. And now I am back to my old self."

"I spent four cents on you!" cried the old man angrily. "I want my money back. I am taking you back to the market to sell you as firewood."

"Very well," said Pinocchio. And then Pinocchio surprised the man as he turned and dove back into the sea.

Chapter 18

I am sure you remember Pinocchio was a very good swimmer, and within minutes he had gone so far he could not be seen. After some time, Pinocchio, still swimming, came upon what he thought was a large rock in the middle of the sea. High on the rock stood a little Goat, who called out to the Marionette.

There was something very strange about that little Goat. Her coat was not white or black or brown, but blue, a deep blue that reminded Pinocchio of his wonderful Fairy.

As Pinocchio swam toward the goat, as quickly as he could, a terrible sea monster came up from the water, with a very large head with a huge mouth, which was wide open.

Do you know what it was?

That sea monster was the very large shark Pinocchio had heard about! Poor Pinocchio! The sight of that monster scared him! He tried to swim away from him, but the shark kept coming closer.

"Pinocchio! Come to me!" said the goat. "Quick, Pinocchio, the monster is close!"

Pinocchio swam faster and faster. He was not quick enough. Suddenly, the monster picked him up, and Pinocchio was in between the shark's white teeth. He drank Pinocchio in, and swallowed Pinocchio, sending him deep into his body.

When Pinocchio recovered from being swallowed, he could not remember what had happened. He looked around and saw nothing but the black night. He heard nothing. He

CHAPTER 18

felt a wind on his face. Slowly, his memory returned, and he realized the wind was from the shark's breathing, and that he was in the shark's stomach.

At first, Pinocchio tried to be brave. But the more he thought about where he was, the more upset he became, and he burst into tears, crying, "Help! Help! Won't someone save me?"

"Who can help you, boy?" said a man's voice.

"Who is talking?" asked Pinocchio, now even more scared than before.

"I am a fish swallowed by the shark at the same time as you. What kind of fish are you?"

"I am not a fish. I am a Marionette," answered Pinocchio, slowly. "What should we do? Can we escape? Is this shark that followed us very long?"

"His body, not counting the tail, is almost a mile long," the fish answered.

Pinocchio looked around, and saw a light in the distance.

"What is that?" Pinocchio asked, pointing toward the light.

"Probably some other fish, waiting like us."

"I am going to go to it—perhaps he knows of an escape."

"I wish you all good luck, dear Marionette."

Chapter 19

Pinocchio began to swim toward the light. What do you think he discovered? You will never guess. He saw a little table set for dinner, lit by a candle. Near the table sat a little old man, eating fish. Pinocchio was so happy, he could not believe his luck. He wanted to cry out, but he discovered he was so surprised, and so happy, that he could not speak. At last, with great effort, he let out a scream of joy and threw his arms around the old man's neck.

"Oh, Father, dear Father! Is it really you? I shall never leave you again!"

"Could it be?" the old man said. "Are you really my boy, my Pinocchio?"

The Adventures of Pinocchio

"Yes, yes! It is I! Look at me! Oh, Father, if only you knew what I have been through. All of the bad things that have happened to me! How I have missed you!"

"I have missed you, too. When I fell out of the boat and into the sea, I wanted to go to you, but the sea was so rough! This terrible shark came up out of the sea, and he swallowed me up! I have been in here for two long years! It has felt like two centuries."

"How have you lived?" asked Pinocchio. Where did you find this candle? And the matches to light it with?"

"Well, the storm that took my boat was also swallowed by this shark. Lucky for me, it was filled with meat, crackers, bread, wine, cheese, coffee, sugar, candles, and boxes of matches. I have been able to live well for two whole years, but now have almost nothing left. And this candle you see here is my very

CHAPTER 19

last candle. I am afraid I am reaching the very end," said Geppetto, sadly.

"And then?"

"And then, my dear, we will find ourselves in the dark."

"Then, dear Father," said Pinocchio, "there is no time to lose. We must try to escape."

"But how?"

"Let's run out of the shark's mouth! We can then jump into the sea!"

"But I cannot swim, Pinocchio!"

"That doesn't matter," said Pinocchio. "I am a very fine swimmer. I will carry you. I am strong. You can go on my back, and we will swim to shore. We at least have to try!"

Without another word, Pinocchio took the candle in his hand, lit the way, and said to his Father, "Follow me. Have no fear!"

They walked a long time, through the shark's stomach. When at last they reached

The Adventures of Pinocchio

his mouth, they stopped for a moment to wait for the right time to make their escape.

Now the shark, being very old, had asthma and heart trouble. As a result, he always slept with his mouth open, which was very lucky for Pinocchio and Geppetto. The two stood by, and through the shark's mouth could see the sky, filled with stars.

"It is time," said Pinocchio. "The shark is fast asleep. The sea is calm. The stars have lit up the sky for us. Follow me Father, and we will be ok."

As they tip-toed over the shark's tongue, they tickled his mouth. The tickling suddenly made the shark sneeze very hard. As he sneezed, Pinocchio and Geppetto were thrown far back into the stomach of the monster! To make matters worse, the candle was out! Geppetto and Pinocchio could see nothing. It was completely dark.

CHAPTER 19

"Do not give up," said Pinocchio, with a serious face. "We must try again! We must keep at it!" Pinocchio held his Father's hand. Walking on their tiptoes, they made their journey again back to the monster's mouth. When they came to the monster's tongue, they were even more careful. They jumped over his teeth. And before they took their last jump, Pinocchio said to his Father, "Climb on my back and hold onto my neck. I will take care of everything else."

With Geppetto settled on top of his shoulders, Pinocchio, dove into the water and started to swim. The moon was shining, and the stars lit the sky. The shark continued to sleep quietly, and Pinocchio and Geppetto were free at last.

Chapter 20

"We are saved, dear Father," cried Pinocchio. "Now all we have to do is swim to shore. We can do it!"

Pinocchio swam quickly, wanting to reach land as quickly as possible. Poor Geppetto, however, was shivering and shaking as if he had a fever.

"Have courage, Father!" Pinocchio said. "In a few moments we will be safe on land."

"But where is the shore?" Geppetto said, sadly. He was scared, worried, and shivering. "I see nothing but sky and sea, everywhere I look."

"Remember, Father. I am like a cat. I see better at night than by day," Pinocchio

Chapter 20

replied. He was beginning to feel weak, for it was requiring great strength to carry Geppetto as he swam. But he could not let his Father down.

The shore was still very far away. He was losing his strength. He was not sure how much farther he could go, and turned to Geppetto, and cried out, "Father! Help me! I feel I am dying!"

"What is the trouble?" said a voice, which seemed to call out from the sea.

"It is I and my Father," said Pinocchio.

"I know you. You are Pinocchio. I am the fish you met inside the sea monster. I got away, just like you. I followed your example. It is only because of your courage that I got away from that terrible monster."

"Oh, fish! Can you help us?" Pinocchio cried out.

"With great pleasure," the fish replied. "Hold onto my tail, and I will lead you to shore. You will be safe soon."

They were at the shore in no time. Pinocchio jumped onto land, helped Geppetto, and turned to face the fish, eager to give him his thanks.

"Dear friend, you have saved my Father. I can never thank you enough!" Pinocchio gave him a warm hug, and the fish returned to the sea.

In the meantime, day had dawned.

CHAPTER 20

Pinocchio offered his arm to Geppetto, who was so weak he could hardly stand. "Hold onto me, dear Father, and let's go. We will walk very, very slowly. We can stop to rest whenever we need to. We will find a house or a hut, where they are kind enough to give us a bite of bread, and some straw to sleep on."

They had barely walked at all, when they came upon the very same fox and cat who had stolen Pinocchio's money! The cat, after pretending to be blind for so many years, had really lost his sight. And the fox had no money! He had to sell his beautiful tail in return for some money to buy some food.

"Oh, Pinocchio," they cried. "Give us some alms! We are old, tired, and sick."

"You are false friends!" answered Pinocchio. "You stole from me once before. You will never catch me again!"

"Believe us! Today we are very poor and starving."

"If you are poor, you deserve it! Remember the old proverb which says, 'Stolen money never bears fruit.' Good-bye, false friends."

"Do not leave us!" they cried.

"Good-bye, false friends," said Pinocchio, determined not to listen to them. "Remember the old saying: 'Whoever steals his neighbor's shirt, usually dies without his own.'"

Pinocchio and Geppetto went on their way. After a few more steps, they saw a tiny house. "There's a house. Perhaps we can find some food and a place to sleep there," Pinocchio said to his Father. "Let's go see what's inside."

Chapter 21

They went to the house and knocked at the door.

"Who is it?" said a little voice.

"A poor Father and a poorer son. We have no food or home. Please help us," Pinocchio said.

"Turn the key and the door will open," said the same little voice.

Pinocchio turned the key, and the door opened. As soon as they went inside, they looked around and saw no one. "Who is here?" Pinocchio said, very surprised.

"Here I am, up here!"

Geppetto and Pinocchio looked up and saw a talking cricket!

"Oh, my dear Cricket!" said Pinocchio.

"Oh, now you call me your dear Cricket, but do you remember when you threw your hammer at me to kill me?"

"You are right, dear cricket. Throw a hammer at me now. I deserve it! But please, do not hurt my dear old Father. He has done nothing wrong."

"I will not hurt either of you. I only wanted to remind you of the trouble you and I once had."

"You are right, little cricket. You are more than right. I shall forever remember the lesson you taught me that day. How did you buy this little house?" asked Pinocchio.

"This house was given to me yesterday by a little Goat with blue hair."

"And where did the Goat go?" asked Pinocchio.

"I don't know."

CHAPTER 21

"And when will she come back?"

"She will never come back. Yesterday she went away, making sad sounds. It seemed like she said, 'Poor Pinocchio, I shall never see him again. The Shark must have eaten him by this time.'"

"Were those her real words? Then it was she—it was—my dear little Fairy," cried out Pinocchio, crying. After he had cried a long time, he wiped his eyes. Then he made a bed of straw for Geppetto. He told him to lie down, and said to the cricket, "Tell me, little Cricket, where shall I find a glass of milk for my poor Father?"

"A farmer lives three fields away. He has some cows. Go to him, and he will give you what you need."

Pinocchio ran all the way to the farmer's house.

"How much milk do you want?" asked the

farmer.

"I want a full glass," replied Pinocchio.

"A full glass costs a penny. First give me the penny."

"I have no penny," answered Pinocchio, sad and ashamed.

"Very bad, Pinocchio," answered the farmer. "If you have no penny, then I have no milk."

Pinocchio started to leave. "Wait a moment," said Farmer John. "Perhaps we can make a deal. Do you know how to pull up water from a well?"

"I can try."

"Then go to that well, and see if you can pull up one hundred buckets of water."

"Very well," said Pinocchio.

"After you have finished, I shall give you a glass of warm sweet milk."

"Ok," said Pinocchio.

Chapter 21

The farmer took Pinocchio to the well and showed him how it worked. Pinocchio set to work. Long before he had pulled up 100 buckets, he was tired and weak. He had never worked so hard in his entire life.

"My donkey always brought me my water from the well," said the farmer. "But now my donkey is dying."

"Can I see him?" asked Pinocchio.

"Of course," said the farmer.

As soon as Pinocchio went into the stable, he spotted a little Donkey lying on a bed of straw in the corner. He was weak from being so hungry, and tired from too much work. After looking at him a long time, Pinocchio said to himself, "I know that donkey! I have seen him before!"

"Who are you?" Pinocchio asked the donkey quietly, as he bent over him.

"I am Lamp-Wick," said the donkey, with

the last energy he had. Then, he closed his eyes and died.

"Oh, my poor Lamp-Wick," said Pinocchio, as he wiped his eyes with some straw he had picked up from the ground.

"Why are you so sad for this donkey," said the farmer.

"He was my friend," said Pinocchio.

"Your friend?"

"A classmate of mine."

"What," shouted Farmer John, bursting out laughing. "What! You had donkeys in your school? How you must have studied!"

The Marionette, hurt by the farmer's words, did not answer, but left quietly with his glass of milk to bring to Geppetto.

From that day on, for more than five months, Pinocchio worked for the farmer every day to bring him water from his well. And every day he worked, he was given a

CHAPTER 21

glass of warm milk for his poor old Father, who was able to grow stronger. He also learned to make baskets and sold them. With this money, he was able to buy them both food so that they would not starve.

He even built a chair that had wheels, which was strong and comfortable, so that he could wheel his Father outside on bright, sunny days.

In the evenings, Pinocchio studied. With the money he earned, he bought old school books, and he was able to teach himself how to read. He also learned to write, and little by little, he was rewarded. He succeeded, not just in his studies, but in his work, and after some time, he had enough money that he and his Father were comfortable and very happy. He even saved fifty pennies. With that money, he decided he wanted to buy himself a new suit.

He said to his Father, "I am going to the market place to buy a coat, a hat, and a pair of shoes. When I come back I will be so dressed up, you will think I am a rich man."

He ran out of the house and up the road to the village, laughing and singing. Suddenly he heard his name called, and saw a large snail.

"Don't you recognize me?" said the Snail.

"Yes and no."

"Do you remember the Snail that lived with the Fairy with blue hair? Do you not remember how she opened the door and gave you something to eat?"

"Why of course I do! I remember everything," cried Pinocchio. "Answer me quickly: Where is my Fairy? Do you know? What is she doing? Has she forgiven me? Does she remember me? Does she still love me? May I see her?"

Chapter 21

All of these questions came quickly, but the snail answered, as calm and slow as ever, "My dear Pinocchio. Your Fairy is very sick. She is lying in a hospital."

"In a hospital?"

"Yes. She is sick and doesn't have a penny with which to buy even a bite of bread."

"Oh no! My poor, dear little Fairy! I have fifty pennies. Here, take them. I was going to buy a new suit, but take them, little snail, and please bring them to my Fairy."

"What about the new clothes?"

"That doesn't matter. What matters is that I help her. I would much rather wear these old clothes and know I can help her than have a new suit. Go! Hurry! Please come back in a few days, and I will bring what other money I earn. I hope to see you soon."

When Pinocchio returned home, his Father asked him:

"And where is the new suit?"

"I couldn't find one that fit me. I will go back to look another day."

That night, after Geppetto fell asleep, Pinocchio made sixteen baskets instead of eight, so that he could give the extra money to the snail. He had to help his Fairy!

Chapter 22

In bed, tired from all his work, he dreamed of his Fairy, beautiful, smiling, and happy, who kissed him and said to him, "Bravo, Pinocchio! As a reward for your kind heart, I forgive you for all of your old mischief. Boys who love and take good care of their parents when they are old and sick deserve praise, even though they may not have always been good. Keep on doing things as well as you are now, and you will be happy."

At that very moment, Pinocchio woke up and opened his eyes.

Imagine his surprise and joy, when, on looking at himself, he saw he was no longer a Marionette, but a real live boy! He looked all about the house, and instead of the usual walls of straw, he saw that he was in a beautiful room, filled with real furniture. He jumped out of a real bed, and saw on a chair nearby a new suit, a new hat, and a new pair of shoes!

He quickly got dressed, put his hands in his pockets, and pulled out a note pinned to a little bag that read:

The Fairy with Blue Hair returns
fifty pennies to her dear Pinocchio
with many thanks for his kind heart.

Pinocchio opened the bag, and guess what he discovered inside? Fifty gold coins!

He ran to the mirror, and he could hardly recognize himself. He had the bright face of a tall boy, with blue eyes, dark brown hair, and a beautiful, smiling mouth. He rubbed his

CHAPTER 22

eyes, to make sure he was not dreaming.

"Oh!" he cried. "Where is Father?" He ran into the next room, and there stood Geppetto! It was as if he'd grown years younger. He was in new clothes, and happy as can be. He was once more like his old self, the wood carver, hard at work on a lovely picture frame, filled with carvings of flowers and leaves and animals.

"Father, Father, what has happened?" cried Pinocchio, as he ran and threw his arms around his Father's neck.

"All of this is because of you, my dear Pinocchio," answered Geppetto.

"Me? Why because of me?"

"When bad boys become good and kind, they have the ability to make their homes bright and new with happiness."

"I wonder where my old self is—the old Pinocchio, made of wood?"

Geppetto pointed to a corner, where a large Marionette, made of wood, sat against a chair. His head was turned to the side, his arms hung with no life. His legs bent under him.

"How silly I was as a Marionette! And how happy I am now," he cried with joy. "Now that I am a real boy!"

Word List

- 本文で使われている全ての語を掲載しています（LEVEL 1、2）。ただし、LEVEL 3以上は、中学校レベルの語を含みません。
- 語形が規則変化する語の見出しは原形で示しています。不規則変化語は本文中で使われている形になっています。
- 一般的な意味を紹介していますので、一部の語で本文で実際に使われている品詞や意味と合っていないことがあります。
- 品詞は以下のように示しています。

名 名詞	代 代名詞	形 形容詞	副 副詞	動 動詞	助 助動詞
前 前置詞	接 接続詞	間 間投詞	冠 冠詞	略 略語	俗 俗語
頭 接頭語	尾 接尾語	記 記号	関 関係代名詞		

A

- □ **a** 冠 ①1つの, 1人の, ある ②〜につき
- □ **ability** 名 できること, (〜する)能力
- □ **able** 形 ①《be – to 〜》(人が)〜することができる ②能力のある
- □ **about** 副 ①およそ, 約 ②まわりに, あたりに 前 ①〜について ②〜のまわりに[の]
- □ **above** 前 〜の上に
- □ **accept** 動 受け入れる
- □ **accident** 名 (不慮の)事故
- □ **across** 前 (身体の一部に)かけて
- □ **activity** 名 活動, 活気
- □ **actually** 副 実は, 実際は
- □ **add** 動 言い添える
- □ **adventure** 名 冒険
- □ **advice** 名 忠告, 助言
- □ **afraid** 形 心配して, 恐れて
- □ **after** 前 ①〜の後に[で], 〜の次に ②《前後に名詞がきて》次々に〜, 何度も〜《反復・継続を表す》副 後に[で] 接 (〜した)後に[で] after all やはり, 何しろ〜なのだから after

that その後
- □ **again** 副 再び, もう一度
- □ **against** 前 〜にもたれて against the wall 壁を背にして
- □ **age** 名 年齢 old age 老後
- □ **ago** 副 〜前に
- □ **agree** 動 同意する
- □ **aid** 名 助け come to someone's aid (人)の救助に向かう
- □ **alive** 形 ①生きている ②生き生きとした
- □ **all** 形 すべての, 〜中 代 全部, すべて(のもの[人]) 名 全体 副 まったく, すっかり after all やはり, 何しろ〜なのだから all at once 突然 all day 一日中 all kinds of さまざまな, あらゆる種類の all night long 一晩中 all over 〜中で, 〜の至る所で, 全て終わって all the way ずっと, はるばる for all 〜 〜にもかかわらず not 〜 at all 少しも[全然]〜ない
- □ **allow** 動 許す, 《– … to 〜》…が〜するのを可能にする
- □ **almost** 副 ほとんど, もう少しで(〜するところ)
- □ **alms** 名 施し(物)
- □ **alone** 副 ひとりで, 〜だけで

110

WORD LIST

- [ ] **along** 前 〜に沿って **along the way** 途中で

- [ ] **already** 副 すでに, もう

- [ ] **also** 副 〜も (また), 〜も同様に

- [ ] **although** 接 〜だけれども, 〜にもかかわらず

- [ ] **always** 副 いつも, 常に

- [ ] **am** 動 〜である, (〜に) いる [ある] 《主語がIのときのbeの現在形》

- [ ] **an** 冠 ①1つの, 1人の, ある ②〜につき

- [ ] **and** 接 ①そして, 〜と… ②《同じ語を結んで》ますます (して)それで, だから **and yet** それなのに, それにもかかわらず

- [ ] **anger** 名 怒り

- [ ] **angrily** 副 怒って, 腹立たしげに

- [ ] **angry** 形 怒って, 腹を立てて **get angry** 腹を立てる

- [ ] **animal** 名 動物 形 動物の

- [ ] **another** 形 ①もう1つ[1人]の ②別の 代 ①もう1つ[1人] ②別のもの **at one time or another** ある時期に **one another** お互い

- [ ] **answer** 動 答える, 応じる 名 答え, 返事

- [ ] **any** 形 ①《疑問文で》何か, いくつかの ②《否定文で》何も, 少しも (〜ない) ③《肯定文で》どの〜も 代 《否定文で》少しも, 何も [誰も] 〜ない **any better** 少しでもよい

- [ ] **anyone** 代 《否定文で》誰も (〜ない)

- [ ] **anything** 代 ①《疑問文で》何か ②《否定文で》何も

- [ ] **appear** 動 現れる

- [ ] **are** 動 〜である, (〜に) いる [ある] 《主語がyou, we, theyまたは複数名詞のときのbeの現在形》

- [ ] **arm** 名 腕

- [ ] **around** 副 まわりに, あちこちに 前 〜のまわりに, 〜のあちこちに

- [ ] **arrive** 動 到着する

- [ ] **as** 接 ①《as 〜 asの形で》…と同じくらい〜 ②〜のとおりに, 〜のように ③〜しながら, 〜しているときに ④〜するにつれて, 〜にしたがって ⑤〜なので ⑥〜だけれども ⑦〜する限りでは 前 ①〜として (の) ②〜の時 副 同じくらい 代 ①〜のような ②〜だが **as a result** その結果 (として) **as ever** 相変わらず, これまでのように **as if** あたかも〜のように, まるで〜みたいに **as soon as** 〜するとすぐ, 〜するや否や **as well as** 〜と同様に **as 〜 as ever** 相変わらず **as 〜 as one can** できる限り〜 **as 〜 as possible** できるだけ〜 **just as** (ちょうど) であろうとおり **twice as long** 2倍の長さ

- [ ] **ashamed** 形 恥じた, 気が引けた

- [ ] **ask** 動 ①尋ねる, 聞く ②頼む, 求める

- [ ] **asleep** 形 眠って (いる状態の) 副 眠って, 休止して **fall asleep** 眠り込む, 寝入る **fast asleep** ぐっすり眠っている

- [ ] **asthma** 名 ぜんそく

- [ ] **at** 前 ①《場所・時》〜に[で] ②《目標・方向》〜に[を], 〜に向かって ③《原因・理由》〜を見て[聞いて・知って] ④〜に従事して, 〜の状態で **at first** 最初は, 初めのうちは **at home** 自宅で, 在宅して **at last** ついに, とうとう **at least** 少なくとも **at one time or another** ある時期に **at that moment** その瞬間に **at the sight of** 〜を見るとすぐに **not 〜 at all** 少しも [全然] 〜ない

- [ ] **ate** 動 eat (食べる) の過去

- [ ] **audience** 名 聴衆

- [ ] **away** 副 離れて, 遠くに, 去って, わきに 形 離れた **far away** 遠く離れて **right away** すぐに

THE ADVENTURES OF PINOCCHIO

B

- **back** 图背中 副①戻って ②後ろへ[に] 形裏の, 後ろの **come back** 戻る **get ~ back** ～を取り返す[戻す] **give back** (～を)返す **go back to** ～に帰る[戻る]
- **bad** 形①悪い ②気の毒な ③(程度が)ひどい, 激しい
- **bag** 图袋, かばん
- **ball** 图ボール, 球
- **barely** 副かろうじて, やっと
- **bark** 動ほえる
- **basket** 图かご, バスケット
- **bass** 图スズキ《魚》
- **be** 動～である, (～に)いる[ある], ～となる 助①《現在分詞とともに用いて》～している ②《過去分詞とともに用いて》～される, ～されている
- **beach** 图海辺, 浜
- **bear** 動身をつける
- **beating** 图たたくこと, 鞭打ち
- **beautiful** 形美しい, すばらしい
- **became** 動 become (なる)の過去
- **because** 接 (なぜなら)～だから, ～という理由[原因]で **because of** ～のために, ～の理由で
- **become** 動①(～に)なる ②(～に)似合う ③become の過去分詞
- **bed** 图ベッド, 寝床 **go to bed** 寝る
- **been** 動 be (～である)の過去分詞 助 be (～している・～される)の過去分詞
- **before** 前～の前に[で], ～より以前に 接～する前に 副以前に
- **began** 動 begin (始まる)の過去
- **begin** 動始まる[始める], 起こる
- **behind** 前～の後ろに, ～の背後に
- **believe** 動信じる, 信じている, (～と)思う, 考える
- **below** 副下に[へ]

- **bend** 動腰を曲げる **bend over ~** に身をかがめる
- **bent** 動 bend (曲がる)の過去, 過去分詞
- **beside** 前～のそばに, ～と並んで
- **best** 形最もよい, 最大[多]の 副最もよく 图《the ~》①最上のもの ②全力, 精いっぱい **try one's best** 全力を尽くす
- **betide** 動起こる, 降りかかる
- **better** 形①よりよい ②(人が)回復して 副①よりよく, より上手に ②むしろ **any better** 少しでもよい
- **between** 前 (2つのもの)の間に[で・の] 副間に **between A and B** AとBの間に
- **bicycle** 图自転車
- **big** 形大きい, 大変な
- **bite** 图ひと口
- **black** 形黒い 图黒, 黒色
- **blew** 動 blow (吹く)の過去
- **blind** 形視覚障害がある, 目の不自由な
- **block** 图大きな固まり, ブロック
- **blow** 動 (風が)吹く **blow ~ off** ～を吹き飛ばす
- **blue** 形青い 图青(色)
- **board** 熟 **get on board** 乗る
- **boat** 图ボート, 小舟, 船
- **body** 图体, 胴体
- **bone** 图骨, 《-s》骨格
- **book** 图本, 書物
- **both** 形両方の, 2つとも 副《both A and B の形で》A も B も両方とも
- **bother** 動～の邪魔をする
- **bottom** 图底
- **bought** 動 buy (買う)の過去, 過去分詞
- **bowl** 图どんぶり, わん
- **box** 图箱, 容器

112

Word List

□ **boy** 名 少年, 男の子 **my boy** 坊や 《呼びかけ》

□ **brain** 名 頭脳

□ **branch** 名 枝

□ **brave** 形 勇敢な

□ **bravo** 間 ブラボー, よくやった

□ **bray** 動 いななく 名 (ロバの) 鳴き声

□ **bread** 名 パン

□ **break** 動 壊す, 折る **break out** (戦いなどが) 勃発する

□ **breakfast** 名 朝食

□ **breathing** 名 呼吸, 息づかい

□ **bright** 形 ①輝いている ②快活な

□ **bring** 動 ①持ってくる, 連れてくる ②もたらす, 生じる

□ **broke** 動 break (壊す) の過去

□ **brother** 名 ①兄弟 ②同胞

□ **brought** 動 bring (持ってくる) の過去, 過去分詞

□ **brown** 形 茶色の 名 茶色

□ **brush** 名 茂み, やぶ

□ **bucket** 名 バケツ

□ **bug** 名 小虫

□ **build** 動 建てる, 組み立てる

□ **building** 動 build (建てる) の現在分詞 名 建物

□ **built** 動 build (建てる) の過去, 過去分詞

□ **burn** 動 燃える, 火照る **burn off** 燃え尽きる

□ **burst** 動 爆発する [させる] **burst into tears** ワッと泣き出す **burst out laughing** 爆笑する

□ **bury** 動 埋める

□ **but** 名 しかし (という言葉) 接 ①でも, しかし ②~を除いて 前 ~を除いて, ~のほかは 副 ただ, のみ, ほんの **cannot help but** ~せずにはいられない **nothing but** ただ~だけ, ~のほかは何も…ない

□ **butter** 名 バター

□ **buy** 動 買う, 獲得する

□ **by** 前 ①《位置》~のそばに [で] ②《手段・方法・行為者・基準》~によって, ~で ③《期限》~までには ④《通過・経由》~を経由して, ~を通って 副 そばに, 通り過ぎて **by day** 昼間に

C

□ **call** 動 ①呼ぶ, 叫ぶ ②立ち寄る **call in** ~を呼ぶ **call out** 叫ぶ, 声を掛ける **call upon** 求める, 頼む

□ **calm** 形 穏やかな, 落ち着いた 動 静まる, 静める **calm down** 落ち着かせる

□ **came** 動 come (来る) の過去

□ **can** 動 ①~できる ②~してもよい ③~でありうる ④《否定文で》~のはずがない **Can I ~?** ~してもよいですか。 **Can you ~?** ~してくれますか。 **as ~ as one can** できる限り) ~ **can hardly** とても~できない **cannot help but** ~せずにはいられない

□ **candle** 名 ろうそく

□ **care** 名 世話, 介護 動 ①《通例否定文・疑問文で》気にする, 心配する ②世話をする **care for** ~が好きである, ~を大事に思う **take care** 気をつける, 注意する **take care of** ~の世話をする, ~面倒を見る **take good care of** ~を大事に扱う, 大切にする

□ **careful** 形 注意深い, 慎重な

□ **carefully** 副 注意深く

□ **carry** 動 運ぶ, 連れていく

□ **cart** 名 荷馬車, 荷車

□ **carve** 動 彫る, 彫刻する

□ **carver** 名 彫刻家

□ **carving** 動 carve (彫る) の現在分詞 名 彫刻, 彫刻作品

□ **cat** 名 ネコ (猫)

113

THE ADVENTURES OF PINOCCHIO

- □ **catch** 動つかまえる **get caught** 捕らえられる
- □ **caught** 動catch（つかまえる）の過去, 過去分詞
- □ **celebrate** 動祝う, 祝福する
- □ **cent** 名セント《米国などの通貨単位。1ドルの100分の1》
- □ **century** 名100年間, 1世紀
- □ **certain** 形～とかいう名前の
- □ **certainly** 副確かに, 必ず
- □ **chair** 名いす
- □ **change** 動変わる
- □ **chapter** 名（書物の）章
- □ **chase** 動追跡する 名追跡
- □ **cheek** 名ほお
- □ **cheerfully** 副陽気に, 快活に
- □ **cheese** 名チーズ
- □ **chicken** 名鶏肉, チキン
- □ **child** 名子ども
- □ **children** 名child（子ども）の複数
- □ **choose** 動選ぶ, （～に）決める
- □ **circus** 名サーカス（団）
- □ **city** 名都市
- □ **clap** 動（手を）たたく
- □ **classmate** 名同級生, 級友
- □ **clear** 形はっきりした, 明白な
- □ **clearly** 副明らかに
- □ **cliff** 名断崖, 絶壁
- □ **climb** 動登る **climb on** ～の上によじ登る
- □ **close** 形近い 動閉まる, 閉める
- □ **clothes** 名衣服
- □ **coat** 名上着, コート
- □ **coffee** 名コーヒー
- □ **coin** 名硬貨, コイン
- □ **cold** 形寒い, 冷たい
- □ **come** 動①来る, 行く, 現れる ②（出来事が）起こる, 生じる ③～になる ④comeの過去分詞 **come back**

戻る **come by** 手にいれる **come down** 下りて来る **come for** ～を迎えに来る **come into** ～に入ってくる **come last** 最後に来る **come out** 出てくる **come out of** ～から出てくる **come running over** 走ってやってくる **come to someone's aid** （人）の救助に向かう **come true** 実現する **come up** 浮上する, 水面へ上ってくる **come upon** （人, 場所など）に偶然出会う, 行き当たる

- □ **comfortable** 形快適な, 心地いい
- □ **coming** 動come（来る）の現在分詞
- □ **complain** 動不平［苦情］を言う
- □ **complete** 動完成させる
- □ **completely** 副完全に, すっかり
- □ **contain** 動（感情などを）抑える
- □ **continue** 動続く, 続ける
- □ **cook** 動料理する
- □ **cool** 形冷えた
- □ **corner** 名すみ, 角
- □ **cost** 動（金・費用が）かかる, （～を）要する
- □ **could** 助①can（～できる）の過去 ②《控え目な推量・可能性・願望などを表す》**Could it be ～?** ～かもしれない **How could ～?** 何だって～ なんてことがありえようか？ **could have done** ～だったかもしれない 《仮定法》
- □ **count** 動～を数に入れる
- □ **country** 名①国 ②地域
- □ **courage** 名勇気, 度胸
- □ **course** 熟of course もちろん, 当然
- □ **courthouse** 名裁判所
- □ **cover** 動覆う, 包む, 隠す **be covered with** ～でおおわれている **cover ～ up** ～をすっかり隠す
- □ **cow** 名乳牛
- □ **crab** 名カニ

114

WORD LIST

- **crack** 動（鞭などを）ピシャリと打つ
- **cracker** 名 クラッカー《菓子》
- **create** 動 製作する
- **cricket** 名 コオロギ
- **cross** 動 横切る, 渡る
- **cry** 動 泣く, 叫ぶ, 大声を出す, 嘆く cry out 叫ぶ
- **cup** 名 カップ, 茶わん
- **cure** 動 治療する, 矯正する

D

- **dance** 動 踊る, ダンスをする
- **dangerous** 形 危険な
- **dark** 形 ①暗い, 闇の ②（色が）濃い 名《the ～》暗がり, 闇
- **dawn** 名 夜明け 動（夜が）明ける
- **day** 名 ①日中, 昼間 ②日, 期日 ③《-s》時代, 生涯 all day 一日中 by day 昼間に every day 毎日 one day （過去の）ある日
- **dead** 形 死んでいる
- **deal** 名 取引 make a deal 取引する
- **dear** 形 いとしい, 親愛なる, 大事な 名 ねえ, あなた《呼びかけ》
- **death** 名 死, 死ぬこと to death 死ぬまで, 死ぬほど
- **December** 名 12月
- **decide** 動 決定［決意］する, （～しようと）決める decide to do ～することに決める
- **decision** 名 決定, 決心
- **deed** 名 行為, 行動
- **deep** 形 ①深い ②濃い
- **delicious** 形 おいしい, うまい
- **depend on** ～しだいである
- **deserve** 動（～を）受けるに足る, 値する, （～して）当然である

- **desk** 名 机
- **despite** 前 ～にもかかわらず
- **determine** 動 決心する
- **did** 動 do（～をする）の過去 助 do の過去
- **die** 動 死ぬ die of ～がもとで死ぬ
- **different** 形 違った, 別の be different from ～と違う
- **dig** 動 掘る
- **dinner** 名 ディナー, 夕食
- **director** 名 監督
- **disappear** 動 見えなくなる, 姿を消す
- **discover** 動 発見する, 気づく
- **disobedient** 形 従順でない, 反抗的な
- **disobey** 動 背く, 従順でない
- **distance** 名 隔たり, 遠方 in the distance 遠方に
- **do** 助 ①《ほかの動詞とともに用いて現在形の否定文・疑問文をつくる》②《同じ動詞を繰り返す代わりに用いる》③《動詞を強調するのに用いる》 動 ～をする could have done ～だったかもしれない《仮定法》 don't have to ～する必要はない
- **doctor** 名 医者
- **does** 動 do（～をする）の3人称単数現在 助 do の3人称単数現在
- **dog** 名 犬
- **dollar** 名 ドル《米国などの通貨単位》
- **done** 動 do（～をする）の過去分詞
- **donkey** 名 ロバ
- **door** 名 ドア, 戸
- **dormouse** 名 ヤマネ《げっ歯類の動物》
- **double** 動 2倍にする 副 二重に see double 物が二重に見える
- **dove** 動 dive（飛び込む）の過去
- **down** 副 下へ, 降りて, 低くなって

形 下方の **let ~ down** ~を失望させる

- [ ] **dream** 動 (~の)夢を見る, 夢想する **dream of** ~を夢見る
- [ ] **dress** 動 服を着る[着せる] **dress up** めかし込む
- [ ] **drink** 動 飲む
- [ ] **driven** 動 drive (車で行く)の過去分詞
- [ ] **driver** 名 (馬車の)御者
- [ ] **drop** 動 落とす
- [ ] **drove** 動 drive (車で行く)の過去
- [ ] **drown** 動 おぼれる, 溺死する[させる]
- [ ] **drum** 名 太鼓, ドラム
- [ ] **drumhead** 名 太鼓の皮
- [ ] **dry** 形 乾燥した
- [ ] **duck** 名 カモ, アヒル
- [ ] **dug** 動 dig (掘る)の過去, 過去分詞
- [ ] **dum** 名 ドン, ダン (という音)
- [ ] **during** 前 ~の間 (ずっと)
- [ ] **dying** 動 die (死ぬ)の現在分詞 形 死にかかっている

E

- [ ] **each** 形 それぞれの
- [ ] **eager** 形 熱心な, ~を切望した
- [ ] **ear** 名 耳
- [ ] **earn** 動 稼ぐ
- [ ] **easily** 副 ①容易に, たやすく ②気楽に
- [ ] **eat** 動 食べる, 食事する
- [ ] **eaten** 動 eat (食べる)の過去分詞
- [ ] **edge** 名 端, 縁
- [ ] **effort** 名 努力(の成果)
- [ ] **eight** 名 8
- [ ] **either** 形 どちらの~も 代 どちらも 副 《否定文で》~もまた (…ない)

- [ ] **on either side of** ~の両側に
- [ ] **elder** 形 年上の, 年長の
- [ ] **else** 副 その他に[の] 形 その他の
- [ ] **empty** 形 空の, 空いている
- [ ] **end** 名 ①終わり, 死 ②果て 動 終わる, 終える **in the end** とうとう, 結局, ついに
- [ ] **energy** 名 力, エネルギー
- [ ] **enjoy oneself** 楽しく過ごす, 楽しむ
- [ ] **enough** 形 十分な, (~するに)足る (~できる)だけ, 十分に, まったく **be kind enough to** 親切にも~する **enough to do** ~するのに十分な
- [ ] **enter** 動 入る
- [ ] **entire** 形 全部の
- [ ] **escape** 動 逃げる 名 逃亡, 脱出
- [ ] **Eugene** 名 ユージン《人名》
- [ ] **even** 副 《強意》~でさえも, ~ですら, いっそう, なおさら **even though** ~であるけれども, ~にもかかわらず
- [ ] **evening** 名 夕方, 晩
- [ ] **event** 名 出来事, 事件
- [ ] **ever** 副 今までに, これまで, かつて **as ever** 相変わらず, これまでのように **as ~ as ever** 相変わらず
- [ ] **every** 形 ①どの~も, すべての ②毎~, ~ごとの **every day** 毎日 **every time** ~するときはいつも
- [ ] **everybody** 代 誰でも, 皆
- [ ] **everyone** 代 誰でも, 皆
- [ ] **everything** 代 すべてのこと[もの], 何でも, 何もかも
- [ ] **everywhere** 副 どこにいても, いたるところに
- [ ] **exactly** 副 正確に, 厳密に, ちょうど
- [ ] **example** 名 例, 模範
- [ ] **except** 前 ~を除いて, ~のほかは

WORD LIST

- [ ] **exchange** 名 交換 **in exchange for** ～の見返りに
- [ ] **excited** 形 興奮した, わくわくした
- [ ] **exclaim** 動 (喜び・驚きなどで) 声をあげる
- [ ] **explore** 動 探検[調査]する
- [ ] **extra** 形 余分の
- [ ] **eye** 名 目

F

- [ ] **face** 名 顔, 顔つき 動 対面する
- [ ] **fact** 名 事実 **in fact** 実際には
- [ ] **faint** 動 気絶する
- [ ] **fair** 名 市場
- [ ] **fairy** 名 妖精
- [ ] **fall** 動 落ちる, 倒れる **fall asleep** 眠り込む, 寝入る **fall out** 落ちる
- [ ] **false** 形 にせの, 不誠実な
- [ ] **family** 名 家族
- [ ] **far** 副 遠くに, はるかに, 離れて 形 遠い **far away** 遠く離れて **far from** ～から遠い
- [ ] **farmer** 名 農場経営者
- [ ] **farther** 副 もっと遠く 形 もっと向こうの
- [ ] **fast** 形 (速度が) 速い 副 ①速く, 急いで ②ぐっすりと **fast asleep** ぐっすり眠っている
- [ ] **fat** 形 太った
- [ ] **father** 名 父親
- [ ] **fault** 名 過失
- [ ] **favorite** 形 お気に入りの, ひいきの
- [ ] **fear** 名 恐れ, 不安 **in fear** おどおどして, ビクビクして **with fear** 怖がって
- [ ] **feed** 動 食物を与える
- [ ] **feel** 動 感じる, (～と) 思う **feel bad for** (人) を気の毒に思う **feel**

like ～のような感じがする **feel sick** 気分が悪い **feel sorry for** ～をかわいそうに思う

- [ ] **feet** 名 foot (足) の複数 **jump to one's feet** 飛び起きる
- [ ] **fell** 動 fall (落ちる) の過去
- [ ] **fellow** 名 人, やつ
- [ ] **felt** 動 feel (感じる) の過去, 過去分詞
- [ ] **fever** 名 熱, 熱病
- [ ] **few** 形 《a ～》少数の, 少しはある 代 少数の人[物]
- [ ] **field** 名 野原, 田畑, 広がり
- [ ] **fifty** 名 50 (の数字) 形 50 の
- [ ] **fight** 動 (～と) 戦う, 争う 名 争い, けんか
- [ ] **figure** 名 人[物] の姿
- [ ] **fill** 動 ①満ちる, 満たす ②《be -ed with ～》～でいっぱいである **be filled with** ～でいっぱいになる
- [ ] **final** 形 最後の
- [ ] **finally** 副 最後に, ついに, 結局
- [ ] **find** 動 ①見つける ②(～と) わかる, 気づく, ～と考える ③得る **find out** 知る
- [ ] **fine** 形 ①元気な ②りっぱな, 申し分ない, 結構な
- [ ] **finish** 動 終わる, 終える **finish doing** ～するのを終える
- [ ] **fire** 名 火
- [ ] **firewood** 名 まき, たき木
- [ ] **first** 名 最初, 第一 (の人・物) 形 第一の, 最初の 副 最初に **at first** 最初は, 初めのうちは
- [ ] **fish** 名 魚
- [ ] **fisherman** 名 漁師
- [ ] **fishermen** 名 fisherman (漁師) の複数
- [ ] **fit** 動 合致[適合]する
- [ ] **five** 名 5 (の数字) 形 5 の
- [ ] **flew** 動 fly (飛ぶ) の過去

117

The Adventures of Pinocchio

- ☐ **float** 動 浮く, 浮かぶ
- ☐ **floor** 名 床, 階
- ☐ **flour** 名 小麦粉
- ☐ **flour-covered** 形 小麦粉をまぶした
- ☐ **flower** 名 花
- ☐ **follow** 動 ①ついていく, あとをたどる ②(忠告などに)従う
- ☐ **food** 名 食物
- ☐ **foot** 名 足 set foot 足を踏み入れる
- ☐ **for** 前 ①《目的・原因・対象》～にとって, ～のために[の], ～に対して ②《期間》～間 ③《代理》～の代わりに ④《方向》～へ(向かって) 接 というわけは～, なぜなら～, だから for a moment 少しの間 for all ～にもかかわらず for the rest of life 死ぬまで for ～ years ～年間, ～年にわたって
- ☐ **forest** 名 森林
- ☐ **forever** 副 永遠に, 絶えず
- ☐ **forget** 動 忘れる
- ☐ **forgive** 動 許す
- ☐ **forgiven** 動 forgive (許す)の過去分詞
- ☐ **forward** 形 前方へ向かう
- ☐ **found** 動 find (見つける)の過去, 過去分詞
- ☐ **four** 名 4(の数字) 形 4の
- ☐ **fourteen** 名 14(の数字) 形 14の
- ☐ **fourth** 形 第4番目の
- ☐ **fox** 名 キツネ(狐)
- ☐ **frame** 名 額縁
- ☐ **free** 形 自由な, 開放された, 自由に～できる 副 自由に 動 自由にする, 解放する go free 自由の身になる
- ☐ **freezing** 形 酷寒の, こごえるような
- ☐ **friend** 名 友だち, 仲間
- ☐ **from** 前 ①《出身・出発点・時間・順序・原料》～から ②《原因・理由》～

がもとで **far from** ～から遠い **from now** 今から, これから **from now on** 今後 **from that day on** その日からずっと **from ～ to** ～から…まで
- ☐ **front** 名 正面, 前 形 正面の, 前面の **in front of** ～の前に, ～の正面に
- ☐ **fruit** 名 ①果実, 実 ②成果
- ☐ **full** 形 ①満ちた, いっぱいの ②完全な
- ☐ **fun** 形 楽しい, ゆかいな
- ☐ **furniture** 名 家具
- ☐ **further** 副 その上に, もっと

G

- ☐ **gallop** 動 ギャロップで走る
- ☐ **game** 名 ゲーム, 遊び
- ☐ **gather** 動 集まる
- ☐ **gave** 動 give (与える)の過去
- ☐ **gently** 副 親切に, 優しく
- ☐ **Geppetto** 名 ゼペット《人名》
- ☐ **get** 動 ①得る, 手に入れる ②(ある状態に)なる, いたる ③わかる, 理解する ④～させる, ～を(…の状態に)する ⑤(ある場所に)達する, 着く **get angry** 腹を立てる **get away** 逃げる **get caught** 捕らえられる **get in** 中に入る **get married** 結婚する **get off** (～から)降りる **get on board** 乗る **get out** ①外に出る, 出て行く ②口に出す **get someone to do** (人)に～させる[してもらう] **get tired** 疲れる **get to** ～に達する[到着する] **get up** 立ち上がる **get ～ back** ～を取り返す[戻す]
- ☐ **ghost** 名 幽霊
- ☐ **girl** 名 女の子, 少女
- ☐ **give** 動 ①与える, 贈る ②伝える, 述べる ③(～を)する **give back** (～を)返す **give up** あきらめる
- ☐ **given** 動 give (与える)の過去分詞
- ☐ **glass** 名 ①コップ, グラス

WORD LIST

□ **go** 動 ①行く, 出かける ②動く ③進む, 経過する, いたる ④（ある状態に）なる **be going to** 〜するつもりである **go away** 出かける **go back to** 〜に帰る[戻る] **go free** 自由の身になる **go home** 帰宅する **go in** 開始する **go into** 〜に入る **go off** 出かける **go on** 続く, 進み続ける **go on one's way** 道を進む **go through** 通り抜ける **go to bed** 寝る **go with** 〜と一緒に行く

□ **goat** 名 ヤギ（山羊）

□ **god** 名 神 **Thank God.** ありがたい

□ **gold** 名 金, 金貨 形 金の

□ **gone** 動 go（行く）の過去分詞 形 去った

□ **good** 形 ①よい, 上手な, 優れた, 美しい ②（数量・程度が）かなりの, 相当な 副 よかった, わかった, よろしい **good for nothing** 役に立たない **have a good time** 楽しい時を過ごす **take good care of** 〜を大事に扱う, 大切にする

□ **good-bye** 間 さようなら 名 別れのあいさつ

□ **got** 動 get（得る）の過去, 過去分詞

□ **gotten** 動 get（得る）の過去分詞

□ **gray** 形 灰色の, 白髪の

□ **great** 形 ①大きい, 広大な, （量や程度が）たいへんな ②偉大な, 優れた ③すばらしい, おもしろい

□ **greatly** 副 大いに

□ **green** 形 緑色の

□ **grew** 動 grow（成長する）の過去

□ **ground** 名 地面, 土 **on the ground** 地面に

□ **group** 名 集団, 群

□ **grow** 動 ①成長する, 育つ, 育てる ②増大する, 大きくなる, （次第に〜に）なる **grow -er and -er** ますます〜する

□ **grown** 動 grow（成長する）の過去分詞

□ **guess** 動 推測する, 言い当てる **guess what** 何だと思う？

H

□ **had** 動 have（持つ）の過去, 過去分詞 助 have の過去《過去完了の文をつくる》

□ **hair** 名 髪, 毛

□ **half** 形 半分の

□ **hammer** 名 ハンマー, 金づち

□ **hand** 名 手

□ **hang** 動 かかる, 垂れ下がる, つるす

□ **happen** 動 （出来事が）起こる, 生じる **happen to** たまたま〜する, 偶然〜する

□ **happiness** 名 幸せ, 喜び

□ **happy** 形 幸せな, うれしい, 幸運な, 満足して

□ **hard** 形 ①堅い ②激しい, きつい, むずかしい ③熱心な, 勤勉な 副 ①一生懸命に ②激しく **hard to** 〜し難い

□ **hardly** 副 ほとんど〜でない **can hardly** とても〜できない

□ **has** 動 have の3人称単数現在 助 have の3人称単数現在《現在完了の文をつくる》

□ **hat** 名 （縁のある）帽子

□ **hate** 動 嫌う

□ **have** 動 ①持つ, 持っている, 抱く ②（〜が）ある, いる ③食べる, 飲む ④経験する, （病気に）かかる ⑤催す, 開く ⑥（人に）〜させる 助《〈have + 過去分詞〉の形で現在完了の文をつくる》〜した, 〜したことがある, ずっと〜している **could have done** 〜だったかもしれない《仮法》 **don't have to** 〜する必要はない **have a good time** 楽しい時を過ごす **have to** 〜しなければならない **should have done** 〜すべきだった

119

The Adventures of Pinocchio

(のにしなかった)《仮定法》should never have done 〜すべきではなかった (のにしてしまった)《仮定法》

- □ **haw** 間えー《口ごもったときの声》
- □ **hay** 名干し草
- □ **he** 代彼は [が]
- □ **head** 名頭 keep one's head down 身をひそめて静かにしている stand on one's head 逆立ちをする
- □ **hear** 動聞く, 聞こえる hear about 〜について聞く
- □ **heard** 動hear (聞く) の過去, 過去分詞
- □ **heart** 名①心臓, 胸 ②心, 感情
- □ **heavy** 形重い
- □ **held** 動hold (つかむ) の過去, 過去分詞
- □ **help** 動助ける, 手伝う cannot help but 〜せずにはいられない help 〜 to 〜の…するのを助ける
- □ **her** 代①彼女を [に] ②彼女の
- □ **here** 副①ここに [で] ②《−is [are] 〜》ここに〜がある ③さあ, そら ここ here is 〜 こちらは〜です。
- □ **hey** 間《呼びかけ・注意を促して》おい, ちょっと
- □ **hide** 動隠れる
- □ **high** 形高い 副高く
- □ **him** 代彼を [に]
- □ **himself** 代彼自身
- □ **his** 代①彼の ②彼のもの
- □ **hit** 動①打つ, なぐる ②ぶつける, ぶつかる ③hitの過去, 過去分詞
- □ **hmm** 間ふむ, ううむ《熟考・疑問・ためらいなどを表す》
- □ **hold** 動つかむ, 持つ, 抱く hold in (動かないように) 押さえる hold out 差し出す take hold of 〜をつかむ, 捕らえる
- □ **hole** 名穴
- □ **home** 名家 at home 自宅で, 在宅して go home 帰宅する on one's

way home 帰り道で take someone home (人) を家まで送る

- □ **hope** 名希望, 見込み 動望む, (〜であるようにと) 思う
- □ **hospital** 名病院
- □ **hot** 形熱い
- □ **hour** 名1時間, 時間 in one hour 1時間以内に
- □ **house** 名①家 ②(特定の目的のための) 建物, 小屋
- □ **how** 副①どうやって, どれくらい, どんなふうに ②なんて (〜だろう) ③《関係副詞》〜する方法 How could 〜? 何だって〜なんてことがありえようか? how to 〜する方法
- □ **however** 接けれども, だが
- □ **hug** 名抱き締めること 動しっかりと抱き締める
- □ **huge** 形巨大な
- □ **human** 形人間の, 人の 名人間
- □ **hundred** 名100 (の数字) 形①100の ②多数の
- □ **hung** 動hang (かかる) の過去, 過去分詞
- □ **hungry** 形空腹の, 飢えた
- □ **hurray** 間ばんざい, フレー《歓喜・賞賛・激励などを表す声》
- □ **hurry** 動急ぐ, あわてる 名急ぐこと, 急ぐ必要 in a hurry 急いで, あわてて
- □ **hurt** 動傷つける, 害する 形けがをした
- □ **hut** 名あばら屋, 山小屋

I

- □ **I** 代私は [が]
- □ **idea** 名考え, アイデア
- □ **if** 接もし〜ならば, たとえ〜でも, 〜かどうか as if あたかも〜のように, まるで〜みたいに if only 〜でありさえすれば

120

WORD LIST

- [ ] **illness** 名 病気
- [ ] **imagine** 動 想像する, 心に思い描く
- [ ] **immediately** 副 すぐに, ～するやいなや
- [ ] **in** 前 ①《場所・位置・所属》～（の中）に［で・の］ ②《時》～（の時）に［の・で］, ～後（に）, ～の間（に） ③《方法・手段》～で ④～を身につけて, ～を着て ⑤～に関して, ～について ⑥《状態》～の状態で 副 中へ［に］, 内へ［に］ **in fact** 実際には
- [ ] **inch** 名 インチ《長さの単位。1/12 フィート, 2.54cm》
- [ ] **indeed** 副 ①実際, 本当に ②《強意》まったく
- [ ] **injure** 動 痛める, 傷つける
- [ ] **inside** 形 内部［内側］にある 副 内部［内側］に 前 ～の内部［内側］に
- [ ] **insist** 動 ①主張する, 断言する ②要求する
- [ ] **instead** 副 その代わりに **instead of** ～の代わりに, ～をしないで, ～ではなく
- [ ] **instruction** 名 指示
- [ ] **interested** 形 興味を持った, 関心のある
- [ ] **interrupt** 動 さえぎる, 妨害する
- [ ] **into** 前 ①《動作・運動の方向》～の中へ［に］ ②《変化》～に［へ］
- [ ] **invite** 動 招待する, 招く
- [ ] **is** 動 be（～である）の3人称単数現在
- [ ] **it** 代 ①それは［が］, それを［に］ ②《天候・日時・距離・寒暖などを示す》
- [ ] **its** 代 それの, あれの

J

- [ ] **jail** 名 刑務所
- [ ] **January** 名 1月
- [ ] **job** 名 仕事, 職
- [ ] **John** 名 ジョン《人名》
- [ ] **joke** 動 冗談を言う
- [ ] **journey** 名 （遠い目的地への）旅
- [ ] **joy** 名 喜び, 楽しみ
- [ ] **judge** 動 判断する 名 裁判官, 判事
- [ ] **jump** 動 跳ぶ, ジャンプする, 飛び越える 名 跳躍, ジャンプ **jump around** 跳び回る **jump into** ～に飛び込む **jump out of** ～から飛び出す **jump over** ～の上を飛び越える **jump to one's feet** 飛び起きる **jump up** 素早く立ち上がる
- [ ] **just** 副 ①まさに, ちょうど, （～した）ばかり ②ほんの, 単に, ただ～だけ ③ちょっと **just as**（ちょうど）であろうとおり

K

- [ ] **keep** 動 ①保つ, 続ける ②守る **keep one's head down** 身をひそめて静かにしている **keep on** ～[-ing] ～し続ける **keep one's promise [word]** 約束を守る
- [ ] **kept** 動 keep（保つ）の過去, 過去分詞
- [ ] **key** 名 かぎ
- [ ] **kick** 動 ける, キックする
- [ ] **kill** 動 殺す
- [ ] **kind** 形 親切な, 優しい 名 種類 **all kinds of** さまざまな, あらゆる種類の **be kind enough to** 親切にも～する **be kind to** ～に親切である **be very kind of you** ～してくださってありがとう
- [ ] **kiss** 動 キスする
- [ ] **knee** 名 ひざ
- [ ] **knew** 動 know（知っている）の過去
- [ ] **knock** 動 ノックする, たたく 名 打つこと, 戸をたたくこと［音］

121

The Adventures of Pinocchio

□ **know** 動 ①知っている, 知る, (〜が) わかる, 理解している ②知り合いである **know nothing of** 〜のことを知らない **know of** 〜について知っている

□ **known** 動 know (知っている) の過去分詞 形 知られた

L

□ **lame** 形 足が不自由な

□ **Lamp-wick** 名 ランプウィック《人名》

□ **land** 名 ①陸地, 土地 ②国, 領域

□ **large** 形 大きい, 広い

□ **last** 形《the 〜》最後の 副 最後に 名《the 〜》最後 (のもの) **at last** ついに, とうとう

□ **late** 形 遅い 副 遅れて, 遅く

□ **later** 形 もっと遅い, もっと後の 副 後で, 後ほど **sooner or later** 遅かれ早かれ

□ **laugh** 動 笑う **burst out laughing** 爆笑する

□ **laughter** 名 笑い (声)

□ **lay** 動 lie (横たわる) の過去

□ **laziness** 名 怠惰

□ **lazy** 形 怠惰な, 無精な

□ **lead** 動 導く, (道などが) 通じる **lead to** 〜に至る, 〜に通じる

□ **leaf** 名 葉

□ **learn** 動 学ぶ, 教わる, 知識 [経験] を得る

□ **least** 形 いちばん小さい, 最も少ない **at least** 少なくとも

□ **leave** 動 ①出発する, 去る ②残す, 〜を見捨てる ③ (〜を…の) ままにしておく

□ **leaves** 名 leaf (葉) の複数

□ **led** 動 lead (導く) の過去, 過去分詞

□ **left** 動 leave (去る, 〜をあとに残す)

の過去, 過去分詞

□ **leg** 名 脚

□ **lesson** 名 教訓, 戒め

□ **let** 動 (人に〜) させる, (〜するのを) 許す, (〜をある状態に) する **let out** 発する **let us** どうか私たちに〜させてください **let 〜 down** 〜を失望させる

□ **liar** 名 うそつき

□ **lie** 動 ①うそをつく ②横たわる, 寝る 名 うそ, 詐欺 **lie down** 横になる **tell a lie** うそをつく

□ **life** 名 ①生命 ②一生, 人生 ③生活, 暮らし **for the rest of life** 死ぬまで **run for one's life** 死に物狂いで走る

□ **light** 名 光, 明かり 動 火をつける, 照らす

□ **like** 動 好む, 好きである 前 〜に似ている, 〜のような 形 似ている, 〜のような 接 あたかも〜のように **feel like** 〜のような感じがする **like this** このような, こんなふうに **look like** 〜のように見える, 〜に似ている **sound like** 〜のように聞こえる

□ **listen** 動《 – to》〜を聞く, 〜に耳を傾ける

□ **lit** 動 light (火をつける) の過去, 過去分詞

□ **little** 形 ①小さい, 幼い ②少しの, 短い ③ほとんど〜ない, 《a 〜》少しはある 副 全然〜ない, 《a 〜》少しはある **little by little** 少しずつ

□ **live** 動 住む, 暮らす, 生きている 形 生きている, 生きた

□ **long** 形 ①長い, 長期の ② 《長さ・距離・時間などを示す語句を伴って》〜の長さ [距離・時間] の 副 長い間, ずっと **all night long** 一晩中 **long before** 〜よりずっと以前に **no longer** もはや〜でない [〜しない] **twice as long** 2倍の長さ

□ **look** 動 ①見る ② (〜に) 見える, (〜の) 顔つきをする ③注意する ④《間投詞のように》ほら, ねえ **look**

WORD LIST

about あたりを見回す **look around** まわりを見回す **look for** ～を探す **look like** ～のように見える，～に似ている **look out** 外を見る **look up** 見上げる，調べる

☐ **lose** 動 ①失う，迷う ②負ける，失敗する **lose one's way** 道に迷う **lose out** 失敗する，大損する

☐ **lost** 動 lose（失う）の過去，過去分詞

☐ **loud** 形 騒がしい 副 大きな音で

☐ **loudly** 副 大声で，騒がしく

☐ **love** 名 愛する人，君《親しい呼びかけ》動 愛する，大好きである

☐ **lovely** 形 愛らしい，美しい，すばらしい

☐ **loving** 形 愛情のこもった

☐ **luck** 名 運，幸運

☐ **luckily** 副 運よく，幸いにも

☐ **lucky** 形 幸運な **lucky for**（人）にとってラッキーだったことには

☐ **lying** 動 lie（うそをつく・横たわる）の現在分詞

M

☐ **made** 動 make（作る）の過去，過去分詞 形 作った，作られた

☐ **maiden** 名 乙女

☐ **make** 動 ①作る，得る ②行う，（～に）なる ③（～を…に）する，（～を…）させる **be made of** ～でできて［作られて］いる **make a mistake** 間違いをする **make money** お金を儲ける **make over** 作り直す **make sure** 確かめる，確認する **make up one's mind** 決心する

☐ **man** 名 男性，人

☐ **manager** 名 支配人，監督

☐ **manner** 名《-s》行儀，作法

☐ **many** 形 多数の，たくさんの **so many** 非常に多くの

☐ **march** 動 前進する

☐ **marionette** 名 操り人形

☐ **market** 名 市場，マーケット

☐ **married** 形 結婚した **get married** 結婚する

☐ **master** 名 主人，所有者

☐ **match** 名 マッチ（棒）

☐ **matter** 名 問題 動《主に疑問文・否定文で》重要である **not matter** 問題にならない

☐ **may** 動 ①～かもしれない ②～してもよい，～できる **May I ～?** ～してもよいですか。

☐ **me** 代 私を[に]

☐ **meal** 名 食事

☐ **mean** 動 ①（～のつもりで）言う，意図する ②～するつもりである

☐ **meant** 動 mean（意味する）の過去，過去分詞

☐ **meantime** 名 合間，その間 **in the meantime** そうこうしているうちに，当分は

☐ **meat** 名 肉

☐ **medicine** 名 薬

☐ **meet** 動 会う

☐ **memory** 名 記憶（力）

☐ **men** 名 man（男性）の複数

☐ **met** 動 meet（会う）の過去，過去分詞

☐ **middle** 名 中間，最中 **in the middle of** ～の真ん中［中ほど］に

☐ **midnight** 名 夜の12時，真夜中

☐ **mile** 名 マイル《長さの単位。1,609m》

☐ **milk** 名 牛乳，ミルク

☐ **mind** 名 心，考え 動 気にする **Never mind.** 気にするな。 **make up one's mind** 決心する

☐ **mine** 代 私のもの

☐ **minute** 名 ①（時間の）分 ②ちょっとの間

123

THE ADVENTURES OF PINOCCHIO

- [ ] **mirror** 名 鏡
- [ ] **mischief** 名 いたずら, (損)害
- [ ] **mischief-maker** 名 いたずらっ子, 故意に問題を起こす人
- [ ] **mischievous** 形 (社会などに)害を及ぼす
- [ ] **miss** 動 (人が)いなくてさびしく思う
- [ ] **mistake** 名 間違い make a mistake 間違いをする
- [ ] **moment** 名 ①瞬間, ちょっとの間 ②(特定の)時, 時期 at that moment その瞬間に for a moment 少しの間 in a moment ただちに
- [ ] **money** 名 金, 通貨 make money お金を儲ける
- [ ] **monster** 名 怪物
- [ ] **month** 名 月, 1ヵ月
- [ ] **moon** 名 月
- [ ] **more** 形 ①もっと多くの ②それ以上の, 余分の 副 ①とても, さらに多く, いっそう more and more ますます more than ～以上 no more もう～ない once more もう一度
- [ ] **morning** 名 朝, 午前 one morning ある朝
- [ ] **mother** 名 母, 母親
- [ ] **mountain** 名 山
- [ ] **mouth** 名 口
- [ ] **move** 動 動く, 動かす
- [ ] **Mr.** 名 《男性に対して》～さん
- [ ] **much** 形 (量・程度が)多くの, 多量の 副 ①とても, たいへん ②《比較級・最上級を修飾して》ずっと, はるかに too much 過度の
- [ ] **mullet** 名 ボラ《魚》
- [ ] **music** 名 音楽
- [ ] **must** 助 ①～しなければならない ②～に違いない
- [ ] **my** 代 私の my boy 坊や《呼びかけ》

N

- [ ] **name** 名 名前
- [ ] **named** 形 ～という名前の
- [ ] **naturally** 副 自然に, 当然
- [ ] **near** 前 ～の近くに, ～のそばに 形 近い 副 近くに
- [ ] **nearby** 形 近くの, 間近の 副 近くで, 間近で
- [ ] **nearly** 副 ほとんど, あやうく
- [ ] **necessary** 形 必要な
- [ ] **neck** 名 首
- [ ] **necklace** 名 ネックレス, 首飾り
- [ ] **need** 動 (～を)必要とする, 必要である 助 ～する必要がある need to do ～する必要がある
- [ ] **neighbor** 名 隣人
- [ ] **net** 名 網
- [ ] **never** 副 決して[少しも]～ない, 一度も[二度と]～ない Never mind. 気にするな。 should never have done ～すべきではなかった (のにしてしまった)《仮定法》
- [ ] **new** 形 新しい
- [ ] **news** 名 ニュース, 知らせ
- [ ] **next** 形 ①次の, 翌～ ②隣の 副 ①次に ②隣に next to ～のとなりに
- [ ] **night** 名 夜, 晩 all night long 一晩中
- [ ] **nine** 名 9(の数字) 形 9の
- [ ] **no** 名 いいえ(という返事), 否 副 ①いいえ, いや ②少しも～ない 形 ～がない, 少しも～ない, ～どころでない, ～禁止 no longer もはや～でない[～しない] no more もう～ない no one 誰も[一人も]～ない
- [ ] **noise** 名 物音
- [ ] **noisy** 形 騒々しい
- [ ] **nonsense** 名 ばかげたこと, ナンセンス
- [ ] **nor** 接 ～もまたない
- [ ] **nose** 名 鼻

124

WORD LIST

□ **not** 副 ～でない, ～しない **not matter** 問題にならない **not yet** まだ～してない **not … without ～ing** ～せずには…しない, ～すれば必ず…する **not ～ at all** 少しも [全然] ～ない

□ **note** 名 メモ, 覚え書き

□ **nothing** 代 何も～ない [しない] **know nothing of** ～のことを知らない **nothing but** ただ～だけ, ～のほかは何も…ない

□ **notice** 動 気づく

□ **now** 副 ①今 (では), 現在 ②今すぐに ③さて 名 今, 現在 形 今の, 現在の **from now** 今から, これから **from now on** 今後 **now that** 今や～だから, ～からには

O

□ **obedient** 形 従順な, 孝行な

□ **obey** 動 服従する, (命令などに) 従う

□ **ocean** 名 海, 大洋

□ **of** 前 ①《所有・所属・部分》～の, ～に属する ②《性質・特徴・材料》～の, ～製の ③《部分》～のうち ④《分離・除去》～から **of course** もちろん, 当然

□ **off** 副 離れて, はずれて 形 離れて 前 ～を離れて, ～をはずれて

□ **offer** 動 提供する 名 (商品の) 売り出し

□ **officer** 名 役人, 警察官

□ **oh** 間 ああ, おや, まあ

□ **oil** 名 油

□ **OK** 形 大丈夫で, うまくいって 間《許可・同意・満足などを表して。O.K. とも》よろしい, いいよ

□ **old** 形 ①年取った, 老いた ②古い, 昔の **old age** 老後

□ **on** 前 ①《場所・接触》～ (の上) に ②《日・時》～に, ～と同時に, ～のすぐ後で ③《関係・従事》～に関して,

～について, ～して 副 ①身につけて, 上に ②前へ, 続けて

□ **once** 副 ①一度, 1回 ②かつて 名 一度, 1回 接 いったん～すると **all at once** 突然 **once more** もう一度 **once upon a time** むかしむかし

□ **one** 名 1 (の数字), 1人 [個] 形 1の, 1人 [個] の ②ある～ ③《the ～》唯一の 代 ① (一般の) 人, ある物 ②一方, 片方 ③～なもの **at one time or another** ある時期に **no one** 誰も [一人も] ～ない **one by one** 1つずつ, 1人ずつ **one day** (過去の) ある日 **one morning** ある朝 **one of** ～の1つ [人]

□ **only** 形 唯一の 副 ①単に, ～にすぎない, ただ～だけ **if only** ～でありさえすれば

□ **onto** 前 ～の上へ [に]

□ **open** 動 ①開く ②広がる, 広げる

□ **opinion** 名 意見

□ **or** 接 ①～か…, または ②さもないと ③すなわち, 言い換えると **at one time or another** ある時期に **or so** ～かそこらで **sooner or later** 遅かれ早かれ

□ **order** 名 命令, 注文 動 (～するよう) 命じる, 注文する **in order to ～** するために, ～しようと

□ **other** 形 ①ほかの, 異なった ② (2つのうち) もう一方の, (3つ以上のうち) 残りの 代 ①ほかの人 [物] ②《the ～》残りの1つ

□ **ourselves** 代 私たち自身

□ **out** 副 ①外へ [に], 不在で, 離れて ②世に出て ③消えて ④すっかり 形 ①外の, 遠く離れた ②公表された 前 ～から外へ [に] **be out** 外出している, 消えている **figure out** ～であるとわかる **out of** ①～から外へ, ～から抜け出して ②～の範囲外に

□ **outside** 形 外部の, 外側の 副 外へ, 外側に 前 ～の外に [で・の・へ]

□ **over** 前 ①～の上の [に], ～を一面に覆って ②～を越えて, ～以上に, ～

125

THE ADVENTURES OF PINOCCHIO

よりまさって ③〜の向こう側の［に］ ④〜の間 ⑤〜について，〜に関して 副上に，一面に，ずっと 形①上部の，上位の，過多の ②終わって，すんで **all over** 〜中で，〜の至る所で，全て終わって **over and over** 何度も繰り返して

☐ **own** 形自身の

☐ **owner** 名持ち主，オーナー

P

☐ **packed** 形混みあった

☐ **pain** 名痛み

☐ **painted** 形描かれた

☐ **pair** 名（2つから成る）一対，ペア

☐ **pan** 名平なべ，フライパン

☐ **panic** 名パニック，恐慌

☐ **paper** 名紙

☐ **parent** 名《-s》両親

☐ **parrot** 名オウム

☐ **party** 名パーティー，集まり

☐ **pass** 動①過ぎる，通る ②（年月が）たつ ③（試験に）合格する **pass by** 〜のそばを通る［通り過ぎる］

☐ **patient** 形我慢［忍耐］強い

☐ **paw** 名（犬・猫などの）足，手

☐ **pay** 動払う，償う **pay a price** 報いを受ける，つけが回る

☐ **peace** 名平和，平穏 **in peace** 平和のうちに

☐ **peaceful** 形穏やかな

☐ **peck** 動（くちばしで）つつく

☐ **penny** 名①ペニー，ペンス《英国の貨幣単位：1/100ポンド》②《否定文で》小銭，びた一文

☐ **perform** 動演じる

☐ **performance** 名演技，見世物

☐ **perhaps** 副たぶん，ことによると

☐ **person** 名人

☐ **pick** 動（〜を）摘み取る，掴み取る **pick up** 拾い上げる

☐ **picture** 名絵

☐ **piece** 名硬貨，コイン

☐ **pigeon** 名ハト（鳩）

☐ **pin** 動ピンで留める

☐ **Pinocchio** 名ピノキオ《人名》

☐ **place** 名場所，空間

☐ **plain** 形（味などが）あっさりした

☐ **plan** 動計画する **plan to do** 〜るつもりである

☐ **plastic** 名プラスチック

☐ **plate** 名（浅い）皿

☐ **play** 動遊ぶ，競技する 名劇

☐ **please** 間どうぞ，お願いします 副どうか，なにとぞ

☐ **pleasure** 名喜び，楽しみ

☐ **pocket** 名ポケット

☐ **point** 動（〜を）指す

☐ **police** 名《the 〜》警察，警官

☐ **policeman** 名警察官

☐ **policemen** 名policeman（警察官）の複数

☐ **poor** 形①貧しい，みすぼらしい ②哀れな，気の毒な

☐ **possible** 形①可能な ②ありうる，起こりうる **as 〜 as possible** できるだけ〜

☐ **pour** 動降り注ぐ **pouring rain** 土砂降り

☐ **praise** 名賞賛

☐ **prefer** 動（〜のほうを）好む，（〜のほうが）よいと思う

☐ **prepare** 動準備［用意］をする

☐ **pretend** 動ふりをする，装う

☐ **pretty** 形かわいい

☐ **price** 名代価 **pay a price** 報いを受ける，つけが回る

☐ **probably** 副たぶん

126

Word List

- **promise** 名約束 動約束する
  keep one's promise 約束を守る
- **prove** 動(〜ということを)証明する prove oneself 実力を示す
- **proverb** 名 ことわざ, 格言
- **pull** 動引く, 引っ張る pull on 〜を引っ張る pull out 引き抜く, 引き出す, 取り出す pull up 引っ張り上げる
- **puppet** 名 操り人形
- **push** 動押す push off 押しのける
- **put** 動 ①置く, のせる ②入れる, つける ③(ある状態に)する ④putの過去, 過去分詞 put down 下ろす put in 〜の中に入れる put on 〜を身につける put up 〜を上げる

Q

- **question** 名 質問
- **quick** 形(動作が)速い, すばやい 副急いで, すぐに
- **quickly** 副 敏速に, 急いで
- **quiet** 形静かな, おとなしい 名 静寂, 平穏 動静まる, 静める
- **quietly** 副 静かに

R

- **rain** 名雨, 降雨 pouring rain 土砂降り
- **ran** 動 run(走る)の過去
- **rather** 副 むしろ
- **reach** 動着く, 到着する
- **read** 動 ①読む ②(文字が)書いてある
- **reader** 名 読者
- **ready** 形用意[準備]ができた be ready for 準備が整って be ready to すぐに[いつでも]〜できる

- **real** 形実際の, 本物の
- **realize** 動〜に気づく, 〜を悟る
- **really** 副本当に, 実際に, 確かに
- **recognize** 動(人物などに)見覚えがある, 識別する
- **recover** 動 回復する
- **refuse** 動 拒む
- **regular** 形正常な, 普通の, 整然とした
- **relieved** 形安心した, ほっとした
- **remember** 動思い出す, 覚えている, 忘れないでいる
- **remind** 動 思い出させる
- **repeat** 動 繰り返す
- **reply** 動 答える, 返事をする
- **report** 動訴える, 報告する 名 レポート
- **require** 動 必要とする
- **resist** 動(したいことなどを)我慢する
- **respect** 名 尊重, 考慮
- **rest** 名《the 〜》残り 動休む for the rest of life 死ぬまで
- **result** 名結果 as a result その結果(として)
- **return** 動帰る, 戻る, 返す 名 ①帰還 ②お返し in return for 〜に対する見返りとして
- **reward** 名褒美 動〜に報いる
- **rich** 形 金持ちの
- **right** 形正しい, 適切な 副 まっすぐに, すぐに right away すぐに
- **ring** 名 輪
- **river** 名 川
- **road** 名 道路, 道
- **rob** 動金品を盗む rob 〜 of 〜から…を奪う
- **robbery** 名 泥棒
- **rock** 名 岸壁, 岩石

127

THE ADVENTURES OF PINOCCHIO

- [ ] **rode** 動 ride（乗る）の過去
- [ ] **room** 名 ①部屋 ②空間, 余地
- [ ] **rope** 名 なわ, ロープ
- [ ] **rough** 形 荒々しい
- [ ] **round** 形 丸い
- [ ] **rub** 動 こする
- [ ] **run** 動 ①走る ②大急ぎで逃げる 名 ①走ること ②途切れずに続くこと　**come running over** 走ってやってくる　**run after** 〜を追いかける　**run around** 走り回る　**run away** 走り去る, 逃げ出す　**run away from** 〜から逃れる　**run down**（液体が）流れ落ちる　**run for one's life** 死に物狂いで走る　**run into** 〜に駆け込む　**run up** 〜に走り寄る

S

- [ ] **sad** 形 悲しい, 悲しげな
- [ ] **sadly** 副 悲しそうに
- [ ] **sadness** 名 悲しみ
- [ ] **safe** 形 安全な, 危険のない
- [ ] **said** 動 say（言う）の過去, 過去分詞
- [ ] **same** 形 同じ　**the same 〜 as** …と同じ（ような）〜
- [ ] **sank** 動 sink（沈む）の過去
- [ ] **sardine** 名 イワシ《鰯》《魚》
- [ ] **sat** 動 sit（座る）の過去, 過去分詞
- [ ] **Saturday** 名 土曜日
- [ ] **sauce** 名 ソース
- [ ] **save** 動 ①救う, 守る ②とっておく
- [ ] **saw** 動 see（見る）の過去
- [ ] **say** 動 言う, 口に出す　**say to oneself** ひとり言を言う, 心に思う
- [ ] **saying** 名 ことわざ, 格言
- [ ] **scared** 動 scare（こわがらせる）の過去, 過去分詞 形 おびえた, びっくりした
- [ ] **scary** 形 恐ろしい

- [ ] **schedule** 動 予定を立てる
- [ ] **school** 名 学校, 授業（時間）
- [ ] **scream** 名 金切り声, 絶叫 動 叫ぶ, 金切り声を出す
- [ ] **sea** 名 海
- [ ] **search** 動 探し求める, 調べる 名 捜査, 探索, 調査　**in search of** 〜を探し求めて
- [ ] **second** 名（時間の）秒, 瞬時 形 第2の
- [ ] **see** 動 ①見る, 見える, 見物する ②（〜が）わかる, 認識する, 経験する ③会う ④考える, 確かめる, 調べる ⑤気をつける　**see if** 〜かどうかを確かめる　**see 〜 as** 〜を…と考える　**see double** 物が二重に見える　**you see** あのね, いいですか
- [ ] **seem** 動（〜に）見える, （〜のように）思われる
- [ ] **seen** 動 see（見る）の過去分詞
- [ ] **self** 名 自分
- [ ] **sell** 動 売る
- [ ] **send** 動 ①送る, 届ける ②（人を〜に）行かせる
- [ ] **sent** 動 send（送る）の過去, 過去分詞
- [ ] **serious** 形 ①まじめな ②深刻な, （病気などが）重い
- [ ] **seriously** 副 真剣に, まじめに
- [ ] **set** 動 ①置く, 当てる, つける ②整える, 設定する ③（太陽・月などが）沈む ④（〜を…の状態に）する, させる ⑤setの過去, 過去分詞 形 準備のできた　**set foot** 足を踏み入れる　**set off** 出発する　**set out** 出発する　**set to work** 仕事に取り掛かる　**set up** 設置する
- [ ] **settle** 動 安定する, 落ち着く
- [ ] **several** 形 いくつかの
- [ ] **shadow** 名 影, 暗がり
- [ ] **shake** 動 ①震える ②《 – hands》握手する, お手する
- [ ] **shall** 動 ①《Iが主語で》〜するだろ

128

WORD LIST

う，〜だろう ②《I以外が主語で》(…に)〜させよう，(…は)〜することになるだろう

- **shame** 图恥，恥辱
- **shark** 图サメ〔鮫〕
- **she** 代彼女は［が］
- **shelter** 图（最低限の）住まい
- **shine** 動光る，輝く
- **shirt** 图ワイシャツ，ブラウス
- **shiver** 動（寒さなどで）身震いする
- **shoe** 图《-s》靴
- **shook** 動shake（震える）の過去
- **shore** 图岸，海岸
- **short** 形短い
- **should** 助〜すべきである，〜したほうがよい **should have done** 〜すべきだった（のにしなかった）《仮定法》 **should never have done** 〜すべきではなかった（のにしてしまった）《仮定法》
- **shoulder** 图肩
- **shout** 動叫ぶ，大声で言う
- **show** 動見せる，示す，教える 图見世物，ショー
- **sick** 形病気の，むかついた **feel sick** 気分が悪い
- **side** 图側，横 **on either side** 両側に
- **sigh** 動ため息をつく
- **sight** 图①見ること，視力 ②光景，眺め **at the sight of** 〜を見るとすぐに
- **sign** 图①きざし，跡 ②看板
- **silence** 图静寂
- **silly** 形おろかな，思慮のない
- **silver** 形銀製の
- **simple** 形単純な
- **since** 接①〜以来 ②〜だから
- **sing** 動（歌を）歌う
- **sink** 動沈む

- **sit** 動座る，腰掛ける **sit on** 〜の上に乗る
- **six** 图6（の数字）形6の
- **sixteen** 图16（の数字）形16の
- **size** 图大きさ，寸法
- **skill** 图技術
- **skin** 图皮膚，皮 動皮をはぐ
- **sky** 图空，大空
- **sleep** 動眠る，寝る
- **slept** 動sleep（眠る）の過去，過去分詞
- **slow** 副遅く，ゆっくりと
- **slowly** 副遅く，ゆっくり
- **small** 形小さい
- **smash** 動粉砕する，強打する
- **smell** 图①においをかぐ ②かぎつける 图におい，香り
- **snail** 图カタツムリ
- **sneeze** 動くしゃみをする
- **snout** 图（馬などの）突き出た鼻
- **so** 副①とても ②同様に，〜もまた ③《先行する句・節の代用》そのように，そう 接①だから，それで ②では，さて **or so** 〜かそこらで **so many** 非常に多くの **so that** 〜するために，それで，〜できるように **so 〜 that** 非常に〜なので…
- **soft** 形柔らかな，やさしい
- **softly** 副やさしく，そっと
- **sold** 動sell（売る）の過去，過去分詞
- **some** 形①いくつかの，多少の ②ある，誰か，何か 副約，およそ 代①いくつか ②ある人［物］たち
- **someone** 代ある人，誰か
- **something** 代ある物，何か
- **son** 图息子
- **soon** 副まもなく，すぐに，すみやかに **as soon as** 〜するとすぐ，〜するや否や **sooner or later** 遅かれ早かれ

129

THE ADVENTURES OF PINOCCHIO

□ **sorry** 形気の毒に［申し訳なく］思う，残念な **feel sorry for** ～をかわいそうに思う

□ **sound** 名音，騒音 動（～のように）思われる **sound like** ～のように聞こえる

□ **speak** 動話す，言う **speak about** ～について話す

□ **spend** 動①（金などを）使う ②（時を）過ごす

□ **spent** 動 spend（使う）の過去，過去分詞

□ **spit** 動吐き出す

□ **spoil** 動台なしにする

□ **spoke** 動 speak（話す）の過去

□ **spot** 名地点，場所 動～を見つける

□ **squeeze** 動押し込む

□ **stable** 名馬小屋，厩舎

□ **stage** 名舞台

□ **stand** 動立つ，立っている，ある **stand by** そばに立つ，待機する **stand on one's head** 逆立ちをする

□ **star** 名星

□ **start** 動出発する，始まる，始める **start doing** ～し始める **start out** 出発する **start to do** ～し始める

□ **starve** 動餓死する

□ **starving** 形飢えた

□ **stay** 動①とどまる，泊まる ②（～の）ままでいる **stay in** 滞在する

□ **steal** 動盗む

□ **step** 名歩み，1歩（の距離）

□ **stick** 動突き刺す

□ **still** 副①まだ，今でも ②それでも（なお）

□ **stole** 動 steal（盗む）の過去

□ **stolen** 動 steal（盗む）の過去分詞

□ **stomach** 名胃，腹

□ **stood** 動 stand（立つ）の過去，過去分詞

□ **stop** 動①やめる，やめさせる，止める，止まる ②立ち止まる **stop doing** ～するのをやめる **stop to** ～しようと立ち止まる

□ **storm** 名嵐

□ **story** 名物語，話

□ **stove** 名ストーブ

□ **straight** 副一直線に，まっすぐに

□ **strange** 形奇妙な，変わった

□ **straw** 名麦わら

□ **street** 名街路

□ **strength** 名力，体力

□ **stretch** 動広がる，広げる **stretch out** 手足を伸ばす

□ **strike** 動打つ

□ **strong** 形強い，堅固な

□ **struck** 動 strike（打つ）の過去，過去分詞

□ **struggle** 動もがく

□ **stuck** 動 stick（突き刺す）の過去，過去分詞

□ **study** 動勉強する

□ **succeed** 動成功する

□ **success** 名成功

□ **such** 形①そのような，このような ②とても，非常に **such a** そのような

□ **sudden** 形突然の

□ **suddenly** 副突然，急に

□ **suffer** 動苦しむ，（損害などを）被る

□ **sugar** 名砂糖

□ **suit** 名スーツ，背広

□ **sun** 名《the –》太陽，日

□ **Sunday** 名日曜日

□ **sunny** 形日のさす

□ **supposed to** 《be –》～することになっている

□ **sure** 形確かな，《be – to》必ず［きっと］～する，確信して 副確かに，まったく，本当に **make sure** 確かめる，

130

WORD LIST

確認する

- **surprise** 動 驚かす, 不意に襲う 名 驚き **to one's surprise** 〜が驚いたことに
- **surprised** 動 surprise (驚かす) の過去, 過去分詞 形 驚いた
- **swallow** 動 飲み込む **swallow 〜 up** 〜を飲み込む
- **swam** 動 swim (泳ぐ) の過去
- **sweet** 形 甘い
- **swim** 動 泳ぐ
- **swimmer** 名 泳ぐ人

T

- **table** 名 テーブル, 食卓
- **tail** 名 尾, しっぽ
- **take** 動 ①取る, 持つ ②持って[連れて]いく, 捕らえる ③乗る ④(時間・労力を)費やす, 必要とする ⑤(ある動作を)する ⑥飲む ⑦耐える, 受け入れる **take care** 気をつける, 注意する **take care of** 〜の世話をする, 〜面倒を見る **take good care of** 〜を大事に扱う, 大切にする **take hold of** 〜をつかむ, 捕らえる **take off** 〜を取り除く **take out** 取り出す **take someone home** (人)を家まで送る **take 〜 to** 〜を…に連れて行く
- **taken** 動 take (取る) の過去分詞
- **talk** 動 話す, 語る
- **tall** 形 背の高い
- **taste** 動 味わう
- **taught** 動 teach (教える) の過去, 過去分詞
- **teach** 動 教える
- **teacher** 名 先生, 教師
- **tear** 名 涙 **burst into tears** ワッと泣き出す
- **tease** 動 いじめる, からかう
- **teeth** 名 tooth (歯) の複数

- **tell** 動 ①話す, 言う, 語る ②教える, 知らせる, 伝える ③わかる, 見分ける **tell a lie** うそをつく **tell 〜 to** 〜に…するように言う **to tell the truth** 実は, 実を言えば
- **temper** 名 短気
- **ten** 名 10 (の数字) 形 10の
- **tend** 動 〜の面倒を見る, 看護する
- **terrible** 形 恐ろしい, ものすごい
- **test** 名 試験, テスト
- **than** 接 〜よりも, 〜以上に **more than** 〜以上
- **thank** 動 感謝する, 礼を言う 名 《-s》感謝, 謝意 **Thank God.** ありがたい
- **thankful** 形 ありがたく思う
- **that** 形 その, あの 代 ①それ, あれ, その[あの]人[物] ②《関係代名詞》〜である…ところの 接 〜ということ, 〜なので, 〜だから 副 そんなに, それほど **now that** 今や〜だから, 〜からには **so that** 〜するために, それで, 〜できるように **so 〜 that** 非常に〜なので…
- **the** 冠 ①その, あの ②《形容詞の前で》〜な人々 副 《 – + 比較級, – + 比較級》〜すればするほど…
- **theater** 名 劇場
- **their** 代 彼(女)らの, それらの
- **them** 代 彼(女)らを[に], それらを[に]
- **themselves** 代 彼(女)ら自身, それら自身
- **then** 副 その時(に・は), それから, 次に 名 その時 形 その当時の
- **there** 副 ①そこに[で・の], そこへ, あそこへ ②《 – is[are]》〜がある[いる] 名 そこ
- **these** 代 これら, これ 形 これらの, この
- **they** 代 ①彼(女)らは[が], それらは[が] ②(一般の)人々は[が]
- **thing** 名 ①物, 事 ②《-s》事情, 事

131

THE ADVENTURES OF PINOCCHIO

柄

- □ **think** 動 思う, 考える **think of ~** のことを考える, ~を思いつく
- □ **third** 名 第3(の人[物]) 形 第3の
- □ **this** 形 ①この, こちらの, これを ②今の, 現在の 代 ①これ, この人[物] ②今, ここ **like this** このような, こんなふうに
- □ **those** 形 それらの, あれらの 代 それら[あれら]の人[物] **those who ~** する人々
- □ **though** 接 ~にもかかわらず, ~だが 副 しかし **even though** ~であるけれども, ~にもかかわらず
- □ **thought** 動 think (思う) の過去, 過去分詞 名 考え
- □ **thousand** 名 ①1000 (の数字) ②《~ s》何千, 多数 形 ①1000の ②多数の **thousands of** 何千という
- □ **three** 名 3 (の数字) 形 3の
- □ **threw** 動 throw (投げる) の過去
- □ **through** 前 ~を通して, ~中を[に], ~中 副 ①通して ②終わりまで, まったく, すっかり **go through** 通り抜ける
- □ **throw** 動 投げる, 投じる **throw about** 振り回す
- □ **thrown** 動 throw (投げる) の過去分詞
- □ **tickle** 動 くすぐる
- □ **tie** 動 結ぶ, 束縛する **tie up** ひもで縛る, 縛り上げる
- □ **time** 名 ①時, 時間, 期間 ②時代 ③回, 倍 **at one time or another** ある時期に **by this time** この時までに, もうすでに **every time** ~するときはいつも **have a good time** 楽しい時を過ごす **in no time** すぐに **once upon a time** むかしむかし
- □ **tiny** 形 ちっぽけな, とても小さい
- □ **tiptoe** 名 つま先
- □ **tip-toe** 動 つま先で歩く, 忍び足する

- □ **tired** 動 tire (疲れる) の過去, 過去分詞 形 疲れた, くたびれた **be tired from** ~で疲れる **get tired** 疲れる
- □ **to** 前 ①《方向・変化》~へ, ~に, ~の方へ ②《程度・時間》~まで ③《適合・付加・所属》~に ④《- + 動詞の原形》~するために [の], ~する, ~すること
- □ **toast** 名 トースト
- □ **today** 名 今日 副 今日 (で) は
- □ **together** 副 一緒に, ともに
- □ **told** 動 tell (話す) の過去, 過去分詞
- □ **tomato** 名 トマト
- □ **tomorrow** 名 明日 副 明日は
- □ **tongue** 名 舌
- □ **tonight** 名 今夜, 今晩 副 今夜は
- □ **too** 副 ①~も (また) ②あまりに~すぎる, とても~ **too much** 過度の
- □ **took** 動 take (取る) の過去
- □ **tooth** 名 歯
- □ **top** 名 頂上 **on top of** ~の上 (部) に
- □ **touch** 動 ①触れる, さわる ②感動させる
- □ **toward** 前 ①《運動の方向・位置》~の方へ, ~に向かって ②《目的》~のために
- □ **toy** 名 おもちゃ
- □ **trade** 名 取引, 商売
- □ **trap** 名 わな, 策略 動 わなにかける
- □ **travel** 動 旅行する
- □ **treat** 動 扱う
- □ **tree** 名 木, 樹木
- □ **trick** 名 ①いたずら ②芸当
- □ **tried** 動 try (試みる) の過去, 過去分詞
- □ **trot** 動 小走りする
- □ **trouble** 名 ①困難, 迷惑 ②もめごと, 事件 ③病気 **with no trouble** 苦もなく
- □ **true** 形 ①本当の, 真の ②確かな

132

WORD LIST

副 本当に **come true** 実現する

- [ ] **truth** 名 事実, 本当 **to tell the truth** 実は, 実を言えば
- [ ] **try** 動 ①やってみる, 試みる ②努力する, 努める **try one's best** 全力を尽くす
- [ ] **tub** 名 桶
- [ ] **turn** 名 順番 動 ①ひっくり返す, 回転する［させる］, 曲がる, 曲げる, 向かう, 向ける ②（～に）なる,（～に）変える **turn around** 振り向く, 向きを変える **turn in** 向きを変える **turn into** ～に変わる **turn over** ひっくり返す **turn to** ～の方を向く
- [ ] **twelve** 名 12（の数字）形 12の
- [ ] **twenty** 名 20（の数字）形 20の
- [ ] **twice** 副 2倍, 2度, 2回 **twice as long** 2倍の長さ
- [ ] **two** 名 2（の数字）形 2の

U

- [ ] **under** 前 《位置》～の下［に］
- [ ] **understand** 動 理解する, わかる
- [ ] **understood** 動 understand（理解する）の過去, 過去分詞
- [ ] **undone** 形 なされていない
- [ ] **unhappy** 形 不運な, 不幸な
- [ ] **unluckily** 副 不運にも
- [ ] **unlucky** 形 不運な
- [ ] **until** 前 ～まで（ずっと）接 ～の時まで, ～するまで
- [ ] **up** 副 ①上へ, 上がって, 北へ ②立って, 近づいて ③向上して, 増して 前 ①～の上（の方）へ, 高い方へ ②（道）に沿って 形 上向きの, 上りの **up to** ～まで, ～に至るまで
- [ ] **upon** 前 ①《場所・接触》～（の上）に ②《日・時》～に ③《関係・従事》～に関して, ～について, ～して 副 前へ, 続けて
- [ ] **upset** 形 ①憤慨して ②動揺して

- [ ] **us** 代 私たちを［に］ **let us** どうか私たちに～させてください
- [ ] **use** 動 ①使う, 用いる ②費やす
- [ ] **used** 動 use（使う）の過去, 過去分詞
- [ ] **useless** 形 役に立たない, 無益な
- [ ] **usual** 形 いつもの, 普通の
- [ ] **usually** 副 普通

V

- [ ] **vacation** 名 （長期の）休暇
- [ ] **very** 副 とても, 非常に, まったく 形 本当の, きわめて, まさしくその **be very kind of you** ～してくださってありがとう **very well** 結構, よろしい
- [ ] **veterinary** 名 獣医
- [ ] **village** 名 村, 村落
- [ ] **voice** 名 声

W

- [ ] **wagon** 名 荷馬車
- [ ] **wait** 動 ①待つ, 《– for》～を待つ ②延ばす, 遅らせる
- [ ] **wake** 動 目がさめる, 起きる, 起こす **wake up** 起きる, 目を覚ます **wake up to** ～に気付く, ～で目を覚ます
- [ ] **walk** 動 歩く, 歩かせる, 散歩する **walk along** ～に沿って歩く **walk away** 立ち去る
- [ ] **wall** 名 壁 **against the wall** 壁を背にして
- [ ] **want** 動 ほしい, 望む, ～したい, ～してほしい
- [ ] **warm** 形 ①温かい ②愛情のある 動 暖める
- [ ] **warn** 動 注意する

133

The Adventures of Pinocchio

- [ ] **was** 動《be の第1・第3人称単数現在 am, is の過去》～であった, (～に) いた [あった]

- [ ] **waste** 動 浪費する

- [ ] **watch** 動 じっと見る, 監視する **watch over** 見守る

- [ ] **water** 名 ①水 ②(川・湖・海などの) 多量の水

- [ ] **way** 名 ①道, 通り道 ②方向, 距離 ③方法, 手段 **all the way** ずっと, はるばる **along the way** 途中で **go on one's way** 道を進む **lose one's way** 道に迷う **on one's way** 途中で **on one's way home** 帰り道で **way to** ～への道

- [ ] **we** 代 私たちは [が]

- [ ] **weak** 形 弱い, 力のない

- [ ] **weaken** 動 弱くなる

- [ ] **weakness** 名 衰弱

- [ ] **wear** 動 着る, 身につける

- [ ] **week** 名 週, 1週間

- [ ] **well** 副 ①うまく, 上手に ②十分に, よく, かなり 間 へえ, まあ, ええと 形 適当な, 申し分ない 名 井戸 **as well as** ～と同様に **very well** 結構, よろしい

- [ ] **went** 動 go (行く) の過去

- [ ] **were** 動《be の2人称単数・複数の過去》～であった, (～に) いた [あった]

- [ ] **what** 代 ①何が [を・に] ②《関係代名詞》～するところのもの [こと] 形 ①何の, どんな ②なんと ③～するだけの 副 いかに, どれほど **What about ～?** ～についてあなたはどう思いますか。～はどうですか。 **guess what** 何だと思う？

- [ ] **wheel** 名 車輪 動 (車輪のついたものを) 押して動かす

- [ ] **when** 副 ①いつ ②《関係副詞》～するところの, ～するとその時, ～するとき 接 ～の時, ～するとき 代 いつ

- [ ] **whenever** 接 ～するときはいつでも

- [ ] **where** 副 ①どこに [で] ②《関係副詞》～するところの, そしてそこで, ～するところ 接 ～なところに [へ], ～するところに [へ] 代 ①どこ, どの点 ②～するところ

- [ ] **whether** 接 ～かどうか, ～かまたは…, ～であろうとなかろうと

- [ ] **which** 形 ①どちらの, どの, どれでも ②どんな～でも, そしてこの 代 ①どちら, どれ, どの人 [物] ②《関係代名詞》～するところの

- [ ] **while** 接 ～の間 (に), ～する間 (に)

- [ ] **whip** 動 むちうつ 名 むち

- [ ] **whisper** 動 ささやく, 小声で話す

- [ ] **white** 形 ①白い ②(顔色などが) 青ざめた

- [ ] **whitefish** 名 白身魚

- [ ] **who** 代 ①誰が [は], どの人 ②《関係代名詞》～するところの (人) **those who** ～する人々

- [ ] **whole** 形 すべての, 丸～

- [ ] **whose** 代 ①誰の ②《関係代名詞》 (～の) …するところの

- [ ] **why** 副 ①なぜ, どうして ②《関係副詞》～するところの (理由) 間 おや, まあ **Why don't you ～?** ～したらどうだい, ～しませんか。

- [ ] **wide** 形 大きく開いた, 幅広の 副 大きく開いて

- [ ] **will** 助 ～だろう, ～しよう, する (つもりだ) **Will you ～?** ～してくれませんか。

- [ ] **wind** 名 風 **wind up** 結局～になる

- [ ] **window** 名 窓

- [ ] **wine** 名 ワイン, ぶどう酒

- [ ] **winter** 名 冬

- [ ] **wipe** 動 ぬぐう

- [ ] **wise** 形 聡明な

- [ ] **wish** 動 望む, 願う, (～であればよいと) 思う 名 (心からの) 願い **wish**

134

Word List

for ～を望む
- **with** 前 ①《同伴・付随・所属》～と一緒に, ～を身につけて, ～とともに ②《様態》～(の状態)で, ～して ③《手段・道具》～で, ～を使って
- **within** 前 ～以内で, ～を越えないで
- **without** 前 ～なしで, ～がなく, ～しないで **not … without ～ing** ～せずには…しない, ～すれば必ず…する
- **woe** 名 悲哀, 悲痛
- **woke** 動 wake(目が覚める)の過去
- **woken** 動 wake(目が覚める)の過去分詞
- **woman** 名 (成人した)女性, 婦人
- **wonder** 動 不思議に思う, (～かしらと)思う 名 驚くべきこと[もの], 奇跡
- **wonderful** 形 驚くべき, すばらしい, すてきな
- **won't** will notの短縮形
- **wood** 名 ①《しばしば-s》森, 林 ② 木材, まき
- **wooden** 形 木製の, 木でできた
- **woodpecker** 名 キツツキ
- **word** 名 ①語, 一言 ②《one's ～》約束 **keep one's word** 約束を守る
- **wore** 動 wear(着る)の過去
- **work** 動 ①働く, 勉強する, 取り組む ②機能[作用]する, うまくいく 名 ①仕事, 勉強 ②業績, 作品 **set to work** 仕事に取り掛かる **work on ～** に取り組む
- **world** 名《the ～》世界 **in the world** 世界で
- **worried** 動 worry(悩む)の過去, 過去分詞 形 心配そうな, 不安げな
- **worry** 動 心配する[させる]
- **worse** 形 いっそう悪い, よりひどい
- **worst** 形《the ～》最も悪い, いちばんひどい
- **would** 助《willの過去》①～するだろう, ～するつもりだ ②～したものだ **Would you ～?** ～してくださいませんか。
- **wound** 名 傷
- **write** 動 書く
- **wrong** 形 間違った 副 間違って 名 不正, 悪事

Y

- **year** 名 年, 1年 **for ～ years** ～年間, ～年にわたって
- **yes** 副 はい, そうです
- **yesterday** 名 昨日 副 昨日(は)
- **yet** 副 ①《否定文で》まだ～(ない[しない]) ②《肯定文で》まだ, 今もなお 接 しかし, けれども **and yet** それなのに, それにもかかわらず **not yet** まだ～してない
- **you** 代 ①あなた(方)は[が], あなた(方)を[に] ②(一般に)人は **you see** あのね, いいですか
- **young** 形 若い
- **your** 代 あなた(方)の
- **yours** 代 あなた(方)のもの

English Conversational Ability Test
国際英語会話能力検定

● E-CATとは…
英語が話せるようになるためのテストです。インターネットベースで、30分であなたの発話力をチェックします。

www.ecatexam.com

● iTEP®とは…
世界各国の企業、政府機関、アメリカの大学300校以上が、英語能力判定テストとして採用。オンラインによる90分のテストで文法、リーディング、リスニング、ライティング、スピーキングの5技能をスコア化。iTEP†は、留学、就職、海外赴任などに必要な、世界に通用する英語力を総合的に評価する画期的なテストです。

www.itepexamjapan.com

ラダーシリーズ
The Adventures of Pinocchio ピノキオ

2018年3月4日　第1刷発行

原著者　　カルロ・コッローディ

発行者　　浦　晋亮

発行所　　IBCパブリッシング株式会社
　　　　　〒162-0804 東京都新宿区中里町29番3号
　　　　　菱秀神楽坂ビル9F
　　　　　Tel. 03-3513-4511　Fax. 03-3513-4512
　　　　　www.ibcpub.co.jp

© IBC Publishing, Inc. 2018

印刷　中央精版印刷株式会社
装丁　伊藤 理恵
カバー・本文イラスト　Attilio Mussino
組版データ　Berkeley Oldstyle Medium + Berkeley Oldstyle Bold Italic

落丁本・乱丁本は、小社宛にお送りください。送料小社負担にてお取り替えいたします。本書の無断複写（コピー）は著作権法上での例外を除き禁じられています。

Printed in Japan
ISBN978-4-7946-0530-6